Spanish Infantry
of the Early Peninsular War:

UNIFORMS, ORGANISATION AND
EQUIPMENT OF THE LINE AND MILITIA

Gerard Cronin and Stephen Summerfield

Illustrated by Christoph Suhr and Vaughan Funnell

Published in 2014 by Ken Trotman Publishing
Booksellers & Publishers
P.O. Box 505
Godmanchester
Huntingdon, PE29 2XW
England
Tel: 01480 454292
Fax: 01480 384651
www.kentrotman.com

Dedicated by Gerard Cronin to his
inspirational Father and Mother

ISBN 978-1-907417-42-9

Design and Index by Stephen Summerfield

Preface

Of all the armies involved in the Napoleonic Wars, pride of place must surely go to the Early Spanish Napoleonic Army for the vivacious splendour of their uniforms, coupled with their tenacious fighting ability. The latter has often been overlooked and seriously underrated. The Peninsular War would have had a far different outcome without the Spanish Army, let alone the leaders and cadres of experienced trained men that they supplied to the ferocious guerrilla bands. The aim of this book is to address these misunderstandings, by firstly bringing together the visual and written information currently available, as well as detailing the many military achievements of the Early Spanish army of the period.

This book gives the uniform, organisation and equipment of the Spanish infantry of the Early Peninsular War. The attempts for the army to change with the times are evident with the increase in light infantry and the numerous uniform changes. This must be set against the crippling debt caused by the Spanish support of the Americans during their War of Independence and then a series of ruinous wars against Portugal, Britain and France. The riches from Spain's possessions in the Americas were becoming increasingly difficult to obtain especially since the declaration of war on Britain, the destruction of her fleet at Trafalgar and subsequent highly effective blockade of Spanish parts by the Royal Navy.

In 1807, Spain already had an auxiliary corps under La Romana in Denmark and was further committed to three divisions in support of the French invasion of Portugal. This permitted a French Army to enter Spain and supply further troops should Britain become involved in the defence of Portugal. The fractious politics in which various factions supporting Godoy, Carlos IV, and his son Ferdinand gave Napoleon the opportunity to conquer Spain in 1808 whilst the best Spanish troops were outside the country. French forces moved swiftly and secured a number of strategic positions, fortified cities and arsenals. In addition, Napoleon enticed Carlos IV and his heir Ferdinand to France where he imprisoned them. Out of this political vacuum, regional and local Juntas started to organise resistance. Despite the grave disadvantages, the old Bourbon Regular Army fought with great valour and solidity as exemplified by the defeat of the French at Bailén (19 July 1808).

In just five years there were three fundamental changes in 1800, 1802 and 1805 of the uniforms for line infantry, light infantry (*Cazadores*) driven by the realisation that the army needed to update.

The changes in uniform took a considerable time to be implemented and the concurrent use of various patterns of uniform as shown clearly shown by the German artists showing La Romana's Division in Northern Germany.

Acknowledgements

The inspiration for this uniform history on the Spanish Army of the Napoleonic Wars resulted from a spellbinding experience many years ago in the Victoria and Albert Museum reading room. A white gloved reading assistant placed in front of me a rare tome of the combined works of Dr Lienhart and Rene Humbert. In total silence, I feverishly thumbed my way through plate after plate of my favourite historical period, the Napoleonic Wars. When I reached the *España Division de Romana*, my eyes were drawn to the glorious colour and panache of these units. That vision has stayed with me still. This work is the culmination of many years of study to place the Spanish Army in the place it deserves. Who could not admire the resplendent uniforms and the men inspired to fight valiantly against overwhelming odds. *Soldados de España, os saludamos.1*

The informed comments from José Luís Arcón, Dr Pedro de Avillez, René Chartrand, Professor Charles Esdaile, Alfonso García-Cervigón Hurtado, Jerry Lavender formerly of the 17/21 Lancers, Colonel Nick Lipscombe and especially Luis Sorando Muzás and Dr Pedro de Avillez have been invaluable in finishing this volume. The editorial comments and corrections of Richard Brown, Anthony Gray and Miguel Mata have been much appreciated.

We wish to thank Angel Aparicio Albert, Dr. Raùl de la Cruz, Alfonso García-Cervigón Hurtado and Martin Valesquez for their assistance in the translation. The support of Tony Broughton, Robert Burnham, João Centeno, Bill Gaskin, Michael Hopper, Digby Smith, Steven H. Smith and Hans Karl Weiss over the many years of collecting information on the Spanish Army has been very welcome.

We wish to thank Richard Brown of Ken Trotman Ltd., the Lipperheide Collection in Berlin, Miguel Mata and the NGA Archive for permission to reproduce various plates from their collections. We are indebted to Marcus Stein of Napoleon-Online for his kind permission to reproduce the 18 plates of Suhr (1808) from the Commerzbibliothek in Hamburg and the Augsburger (1802-08) plates from the Landes- und Hochschulbibliothek in Darmstadt. The assistance of the Museo del Ejército formally in Madrid and now in Toledo, Royal Armouries Library, the British Library and Loughborough University Library has been greatly appreciated.

Gerard Cronin
Gringo40s

Dr. Stephen Summerfield
Loughborough University
10 February 2014

---

[1] Translation "Soldiers of Spain, we salute you."

Contents

Orders of Battle

Tables

Introduction

00The most important of these sources is the work of Professor Christoph Suhr (1771-1842) on the Spanish troops quartered in Hamburg from 1807-1808. He had been professor in the Academy of Arts in Berlin before returning to his birthplace of Hamburg in 1806. In 1808, Professor Christoph Suhr published a small series of 18 plates depicting La Romana's Division in Hamburg during 1807-08.[2] Then in 1818, he published a complete set of 158 plates depicting 500 different uniforms of troops stationed in Hamburg from 1806 to 1815.[3] These were from the sketches obviously drawn from life by the talented Professor Christoph Suhr then subsequently engraved and hand coloured by Cornelius Suhr. Richard Knötel writing in 1904 considered the worth of Suhr as incalculable because of his exceptional eye for detail and reliability in contrast to the Elberfelder Manuscript drawn by an amateur.[4] Twenty-nine of the fifty-one plates are reproduced in this volume.

The work of the Suhr brothers has been subsequently used by many authors and artists including Lienhart and Humbert (1895), Boppe (1899),[5] Richard Knötel in his *Uniformkunde* (c1900), Funcken & Funcken (1973), Windrow and Embleton (1974),[6] Otto von Pivka (1975),[7] Lachouque (1982), Bueno (1982, 1990 & 1991),[8] Daniel Lordey in Coppens *et al.* (1997) and Herbert Knötel in Elting (2000).

Cazadores de Cataluña
After Christoph Suhr

---

[2] Suhr C. (1808) *Die Spanischen Truppen der Division Romána in Hamburg während der Jahre 1807 und 1808*, Hamburg.

[3] Suhr C. (1818) *Das Brokthor in Hamburg Während der Belagerungszeit 1813-14*, (1820) *Abbildung der Uniformen aller in Hamburg seit den Jahren 1806 bis 1815 einquartirt gewesener Truppen*, Hamburg.

[4] Richard Knötel (1904) *Mitteilungen zur Geschichte der Militärischen Tracht: Das grosse Uniformwerk des Hamburgers Christoph Suhr 1806-1815*, Verlag von Max Bab, Berlin

[5] Boppe P. (1899 rp 1986) *Les Espagnols à la Grande Armée*, C. Terana Editeur.

[6] Windrow M. and Embleton G. (1974) *Military Dress of the Peninsular War*, Ian Allen Ltd.

[7] Digby Smith [Otto von Pivka] (1975) *Spanish Armies of the Napoleonic Wars*, Osprey.

[8] Bueno Carrera, José María (1982) *El Ejército y la Armada en 1808*, (1989) *Uniformes Militares de la Guerra de la Independencia*, (1990) *La Expedición Española a Dinamarca 1807-1808*, (1991) *Andalucía y sus Milicias*, Aldaba Militaría, Madrid.

The almost 100 contemporary lithographs come from the 1805 and 1806 editions of the *Reglamento de Uniformidad del Ejército y la Marina en 1805*. These show the M1805 uniform, although never universally worn even by 1808. The uniform schema are in accordance to more recent research of Bueno (1982, 1990 & 1991) based upon the contemporary work of D. Juan Josef Ordovás *Estado del ejército y la armada* of 1807.[9]

These have been have been supplemented by German lithographic plates of Thomas Weber (1806) and Augsburger (1807-08) depicting the Spanish troops of the Etruria Expeditionary Force. The prints by Bradford (1809),[10] Goddard and Booth (1812)[11] and Perez (1806) depict those regiments left in Spain or recently returned. Their work has been supplemented by the work of Clonard (1851-59) and Boppe (1899).

The superb line drawings by Vaughn Funnell were specially commissioned for this work based upon the work of Bueno (1982 and 1990). The plans of the ordnance, uniform schema and some of the flags were drawn by the authors. Without the work of Luís Sorando Muzás,[12] the design of Spanish flags would be almost impossible to unravel. He also investigated the actual uniforms worn by the Line Infantry on 2 May 1808.[13]

Spanish Grenadier
By Vaughan Funnell

The Campaign Histories were compiled mainly from the Spanish sources of Ordovás (1807), *Estados de la Organización y Fuerza* (Anon, 1822), Arteche (1868-1902),[14] Clonard (1851-59),[15] Bueno (1982, 1989 & 1990), and Sorando

---

[9] Ordovás (1807) *Estado del Ejército y la Armada de Su Majestad Católica formado por el Teniente Coronel del Real Cuerpo de Ingenieros Don Juan José Ordovás, anno 1807*, Madrid.

[10] William Bradford (1809) *Sketches of Military Costume in Spain and Portugal. With a statement of their regulations relative to rank, formation, and force*, London [13 plates]

[11] Goddard T. and Booth J. (1812) *The Military Costume of Europe* ..... [96 plates]

[12] Sorando Muzás (2001) *Banderas, estandartes y trofeos del Museo del Ejército 1700-1843, Catálogo razonado*, Spanish Ministry of Defence.

[13] Sorando Muzás (2012) "La Infantería de Línea Española en 1808," *Miniatures Militares.* (2012) "La Infantería de Línea Española en 1808," *Miniatures Militares.*

[14] Arteche, Gómez de (1868-1902) *Guerra de la Independencia*, Volume I-XIV, Madrid.

[15] Clonard, Conde de (1851-59) *Historia orgánica de las armas de Infantería y caballería españolas*, Volumes V-XVI, Madrid.

Muzás (2007 & 2012). These have been supplemented by the English language sources of Sir Charles Oman (1902-30),[16] Nafziger (1993),[17] René Chartand,[18] Partridge & Oliver (1999)[19] and Digby Smith (1998).[20]

The following conventions have been used in this volume:

- Spanish rank titles and names have been preserved as far as possible.
- Consistency in the spelling of names, places and units has been difficult with the changes in Spanish and Portuguese spelling over the last two centuries as well as English, French, German, Portuguese Spanish sources have been used in this work.
- The *Caballería de Línea* is literally line cavalry in English but has been translated into more familiar heavy cavalry to avoid confusion.
- The Spanish *Cazadores a Caballo* has been preferred to the French version of *Chasseurs à Cheval* or light cavalry.
- *Sargento mayor* did not mean the NCO rank of sergeant major but was a relic of the 16th century when he was the second in command of a Tercio, under a *maestre de campo* therefore he ranked as a major.
- The line infantry and cavalry have been assigned a number according to their seniority in Ordovás (1807) as used by Bueno (1982).
- The Spanish-used measurements have been converted to metric. It is interesting that the Spanish used French weight to define their weight of shot but Spanish measures for the tube length and weight in *libras*.
- Battalions and squadrons are designated by Roman numerals (e.g. I, II, III, IV etc.).
- *Ligne* and *Légère* refer to French line and light infantry respectively. French formations use Arabic numerals (e.g. 1e Corps, 2e Division and 3e Brigade).
- French Generals have been abbreviated as follows: *Général de Brigade* (GdB) and *Général de Division* (GdD).

---

[16] Oman C, (1902-1930), *History of the Peninsular War*, Volume I-VII, London. These have caused much confusion due to inconsistent translation and regimental identification that have been perpectuated by later works in English.
[17] Nafziger GF (1993) *The Armies of Spain and Portugal*, 3rd Edition, The Nafziger Collection.
[18] Chartrand, R. (1998-99), *The Spanish Army of the Napoleonic Wars*, Vol I-III, Osprey and (2011), *The Spanish Army in North America 1700-1783*, Osprey
[19] Partridge R. and Oliver M. (1999) *Napoleonic Army Handbook: The British Army and her Allies*, Constable, London.
[20] Digby Smith (1998) *The Greenhill Napoleonic Wars Data Book*, Greenhill Books.

Plate 1: Captains of the *Regimiento de Guadalajara* and the *Regimiento de Caballería del Rey*

By Christoph Suhr

Suitably attired for their night out on the town, the two captains in contrasting yet elegant uniforms are very interesting in as much as the high waisted jacket of the *Regimiento de Guadalajara* in M1805 white uniform remained virtually unchanged even down to the oversized bicorns. Both officers carry their swords in their hands or under their arms as was common with the Spanish.

Chapter 1
The Spanish Army

From 1582 to 1640, the "Union of Crowns" of Portugal and Spain was the high point of Imperial power. The Portuguese decision to crown the Duke of Braganza in 1640 and once again be a separate state heralded the start of the almost continuous decline in the power of Spain. The accession of Philip V in 1700, a grandson of Louis XIV of France, brought attempts to modernise the army based upon the French model. Numerous officers were trained in French military academies and even saw service in the French Army. After the Seven Years War, Carlos III commissioned Conde de O'Reilly to reform the army upon Prussian lines and this resulted in the Ordenanzas of 1768.[21] The adoption of Prussian drill and to a lesser extent its discipline was strongly resisted by the proud individualistic Spanish soldiers. In battle, they were brave, hotheaded and were at times difficult to control. The Swiss and Walloon Regiments were well known for their steadiness under fire.[22]

Spanish infantry in 1780
[Clonard]

Spain's small well trained and confident army of only 78,000 men had performed well during the American War of Independence (1775-83).[23] However, it became increasingly difficult to continue to supply fresh contingents to the numerous garrisons in her American colonies. In 1776, there were 32 battalions serving

---

[21] Esdaile (1988) p5
[22] Chartrand (1998) I: p3
[23] Chartrand (1998) I: pp3-4

outside Europe and this number rose to 35 in 1782. From the late 1780s, Spanish colonies were permitted to raise their own troops and those from Spain were able to return home. The only garrisons maintained by the Spanish Army were the two presidencies of Ceuta[24] and Melilla,[25] the Balearic Islands in the Mediterranean and the Canary Islands on the northwest coast of Africa.[26] In 1787, the Prussian influence increased with the publication of a treatise on the Prussian military system by Tomás de Morla.[27]

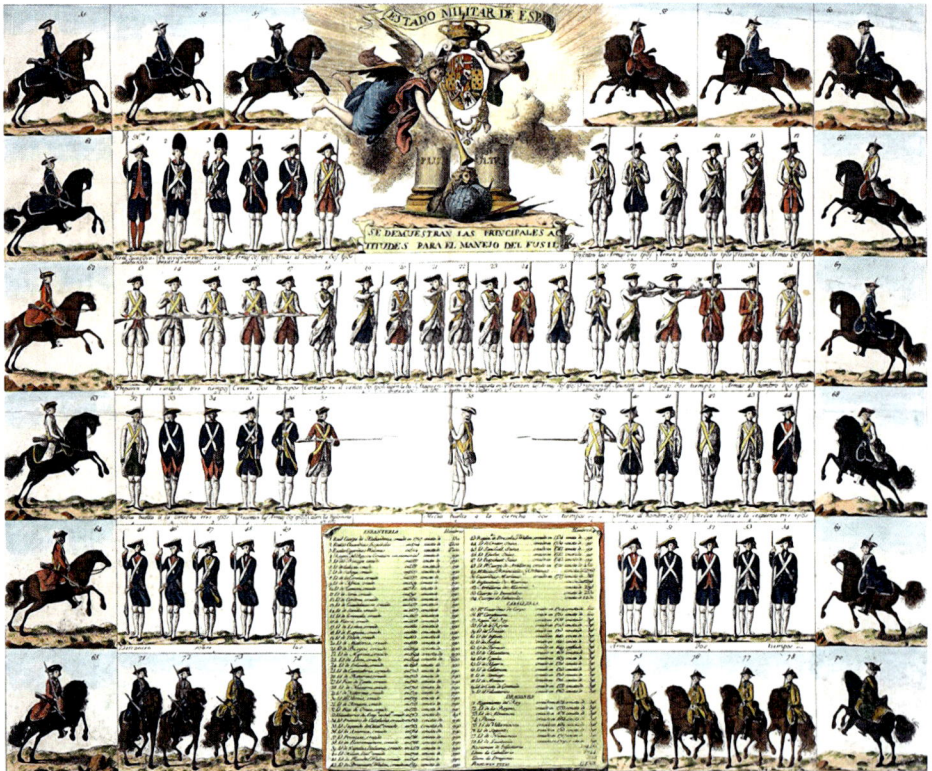

Schema of the Spanish Army in 1780

There was comparatively little change between the end of the War of Spanish Succession and the French Revolution, during which period only two *Cazadores* (light infantry) regiments, three line infantry regiments and four foreign regiments were raised.[28]

The officer corps was of poor quality being noted for their low technical skills, internal rivalry and the high percentage of foreign officers among them. A cadet had to be at least 16 before he could join a regiment. He had to prove his noble

---

[24] Ceuta is located on the north coast of Africa surrounded by Morocco and separated from the Spain by the Straits of Gibraltar.
[25] Melilla is an enclave on the north coast of Morocco.
[26] Laborde (1809) p501
[27] Esdaile (1988) p5
[28] Nafziger (1993) p4

birth to join the heavy cavalry, Dragoons, Spanish and Walloon Guards. Such proof of nobility was not required for the infantry or the technical services. Promotion to officer depended upon the support of his colonel and then approved by the inspecting general. Promotion could take as long as 5-6 years.

NCOs could be commissioned except in the artillery and the Spanish and Walloon Guards. Laborde (1809) estimated that commissioned NCOs made up about half of the officers in the infantry and cavalry.[29] Officers who were nobles avoided field service and attempted to spend their time at court where they could gain promotion quicker than by risking their life in combat. This resulted in the commoners rarely reaching higher than company officers.

The military schools in Cadiz, Barcelona and Zamora taught the principles of design, mathematics, engineering and fortifications. These schools chiefly catered to instruct cadets who were intending a career in the artillery or engineers. Another military school was established by Carlos III (r. 1759-88) in Avila.[30]

Spain was divided into eleven Military Departments of Andalucía, Aragón, Catalonia (Cataluña), Extremadura, Galicia, the coast of Granada, Guipúzcoa, Madrid, Navarre (Navarra), Old Castile, and Valencia & Murcia. The military governors aside from taking the title of Captain General presided over the supreme courts and managed the police force. The Captain General of Navarre added that of viceroy as well.[31]

1808.
TROUPES ALLIÉES. — ESPAGNE.
RÉGIMENTS DE CATALOGNE, DE L'INFANTE ET DE ZAMORA.

---

[29] Laborde (1809) IV: p502
[30] Laborde (1809) IV: p498
[31] Laborde (1809) IV: p491

OOB 1: The Army Staff of 1798[32]

General Officers

Capitánes Generales (Captain-General)	11	
Tenientes Generales (Lieutenant-General)	112	
Mariscales de Campo (Major-General)	137	
Brigadiers	<u>300</u>	**560**

Administrative Staff

Inspector Generals[33] of Infantry, Cavalry, Dragoons, Artillery, Engineers and Militia	6
Intendentes de Ejército (Quartermaster Generals)[34]	10
Minister of Ceuta	1
Veedores (local inspectors)	2
Contadores (Treasury auditors distributed to the provinces)	12
Military Commissaries (15 principal and 69 ordinary)	84
Treasurers of the Army	10
Military Judges	12

TOTAL   **700**

The number of Generals was reduced from 560 in 1798 to 433 in 1807 and to 327 in 1808.

OOB 2: Number of generals in 1807

Capitánes Generales (Captain-General)	5
Tenientes Generales (Lt-General)	86
Mariscales de Campo (Maj-General)	118
Brigadieres (Brigadiers)	<u>198</u>
TOTAL	**407**

Of the 327 generals in 1808, 77 were foreigners.[35] The eighteen provinces each had an *Intendente de Provincia* (Provincial Commandants) who were responsible for the inspection of the provinces.[36]

---

[32] Laborde (1809) IV: pp455-456.

[33] The *Inspector-Generals* oversaw every class of troops of the line and were members of the supreme war council. They carried on direct correspondence with the army, received orders from the king and his ministry then communicated these to the commanders of the different corps and nominated candidates for promotion. [Laborde (1809) IV: pp455-456]

[34] *Andalusia; Aragón, Navarra* (Navarre) and *Guipuzcoa; Caracas; Catalonia; Extremadura; Galicia; Habana* (Havanna); *Mallorca* (Majorca); *Valencia* and *Murcia; Valladolid.*

[35] Nafziger (1993) p5.

[36] Avila, Burgos, Carolina, Ciudad Real, Cordova, Cuenca, Granada, Guadalajara, Jaén, León, Madrid, Murcia, Palencia, Salamanca, Segovia, Soria, Toledo and Zamora. [Bueno (1982) p12 and Laborde (1809) IV: p456]

OOB 3: Distribution of Generals in 1808[37]

Infantería de Línea (Line Infantry)
>1 *Inspector General de Infantería de Línea* (Inspector General of Line Infantry)
>1 *Capitán General* (Capt-Gen), 33 *Tenientes Generales* (Lt-Gen)
>22 *Mariscales de Campo* (Maj-Gen), 34 brigadiers

Tropas Extranjeras (Foreign Infantry)
>1 *Inspector General de Tropas Extranjeras* (Inspector General of Foreign Infantry)
>3 *Tenientes Generales* (Lt-Gen), 2 *Mariscales de Campo* (Maj-Gen), 3 brigadiers

Tropas Ligeras (Light Infantry)
>1 *Inspector General de Tropas Ligeras* (Inspector General of Light Infantry)
>2 *Tenientes Generales* (Lt-Gen), 3 *Mariscales de Campo* (Maj-Gen), 1 brigadiers

Caballería de Línea (Heavy Cavalry)
>1 *Inspector General de Caballería de Línea* (Inspector General of Heavy Cavalry)
>8 *Tenientes Generales* (Lt-Gen), 7 *Mariscales de Campo* (Maj-Gen), 7 brigadiers

Caballería Ligera (Light Cavalry)
>1 *Inspector General de Caballería Ligera* (Inspector General of Light Cavalry)
>3 *Tenientes Generales* (Lt-Gen), 8 *Mariscales de Campo* (Maj-Gen), 8 brigadiers

Artillería (Artillery)
>1 *Inspector General de Artillería* (Inspector General of Artillery), 1 *Jefe de Estado Mayor* (Chief of Staff), 12 *Sub-inspectores Comandantes de Departamento* (6 Generals and 6 Brigadiers), 5 *Jefes de Escuela* (college commandants with the rank of brigadier)

Ingenieros (Engineers)
>1 *Inspector General de Ingenieros* (Inspector General of Engineers)

Milicias (Militia)
>1 *Inspector General de Milicias* (Inspector General of Militia)

**General Pedro Caro y Sureda,
3rd Marquis de la Romana**
Manuel Castallano, 1850

---

[37] Bueno (1982) p12

Recruiting

By 1703, Philip V had established sporadic drafts from quintas (ballots) at times of national crisis but these were ineffective. The army was raised from volunteers, foreigners, convicted criminals given the choice to serve in the army and *levas* (literally levies) upon the unemployed or homeless (known as *vagos*). The availability of suitable foreign volunteers was limited due to the low esteem of the army and poor pay. In addition, soldiers were required to wear full uniform in public, keep their hair powdered and dressed at all times. They were also forbidden to sit or smoke in public and were disciplined by NCOs carrying thick canes.[38]

In 1770, a new system of conscription was introduced. It was known as the *sorteo* and was based upon the Prussian canton system. It brought conscription to the previously exempted Catalonia. This was a response to the threat of war with Britain over the Falklands and the need of Carlos III to rationalise the raising of troops he required for the army. The Decree of 7 November 1770 required that a ballot of registered single men aged 17-36 as well as over 153cm[39] tall to serve in the army would be carried out each year. The exemptions included clerics, government officials, factory workers, artisans, educated professionals, stockbreeders and men of property so the draft fell heavily upon the poor and landless.[40] Service in the army was so unpopular that many young men would avoid the draft by marrying, fleeing to the hills or taking sanctuary in churches. Those who did not were put under guard. So many evaded conscription by marrying that the Decree of 22 June 1773 annulled marriages that occurred less than 15 days prior to the ballot (*sorteo*).[41]

The Decree of 7 May 1775 codified the *leva* (levy) that aimed to purge society of 17-36 year olds who were without permanent employment, suspected criminals and troublemakers for service in the army. The Decree of 13 May 1775 ordered that *levas* were authorised to occur on the same day as the ballot (*sorteo*). Between 1730 and 1789, 24,889 out of 44,777 men arrested as *vagos* were drafted into the army.[42]

The *sorteo* was abandoned in 1777 due to widespread rioting and disorder. Therefore, the army had to return to voluntary enlistment and the *leva*. The Spanish army was just as short of recruits as it had been in 1770. This resulted in the re-introduction of the draft (*quinta*). In February 1793, the unpopular *sorteo* and *leva* were reintroduced. In 1794, generous bounties and the offer of an amnesty to deserters who rejoined their units raised 40,000 men. Despite this, a further *sorteo* was imposed in early 1795 and the conscripts served for the duration of the war.[43]

When war was once more declared against France in June 1808, every local Junta imposed universal service with the exemptions from military service abolished except for Catalonia who persevered with volunteer enlistment.[44]

---

[38] Esdaile (2008) p105; Nafziger (1993) pp4-5.
[39] The Spanish measure was 5 pies 6 pulgadas or 5 Imperial feet.
[40] Esdaile (2008) pp106-107 and Nafziger (1993) p5
[41] Esdaile (2008) pp108-109; Nafziger (1993) pp4-5
[42] Esdaile (2008) p. 109, Esdaile (2012) "The Spanish Army under the Ancien Regime" pp1-2
[43] Esdaile (2012) "The Era of Godoy 1792-1808" pp12-13
[44] Esdaile (2011) p199

Chapter 2
La Romana Division in Northern Europe

In 1788, Carlos IV (1748-1819) succeeded his father Carlos III (1716-88) and attempted to continue with the much needed reforms of his father. The heir to the throne was a weak and vacillating Prince Ferdinand of Asturias (1784-1833). In 1790, the Nootka Crisis brought Spain once again into conflict with Britain over territorial claims over British Columbia but when the French National Assembly refused to respect the alliance with Spain and support her claims so forced Spain to settle.[45] The real power in Spain was Manuel de Godoy (1767-1851)[46] who was chief minister and Queen Luisa of Parma's "favourite."

On 23 March 1793, Spain declared war upon Revolutionary France. Portugal followed suite due to her obligations to the mutual defence treaty of 1778 with Spain and her traditional alliance with Britain from the 13th Century. General Ventura Caro's army of 8,000 men defended the Basque Provinces and Navarre (Navarra). Another 5,000 defended the central Pyrenees. Captain-General António Ricardos y Carrillo with 41 cavalry squadrons, 38 infantry battalions and 150 artillery pieces totalling 24,000 men invaded the French province of Roussillon.

The Spanish Army was reinforced by a Portuguese Auxiliary Division of 5,400 men under General João (John) Forbes-Skelater (1733-1808)[47] which disembarked near the Spanish port of Rosas on 10 November 1793 and protected by a Portuguese fleet of 15 ships. Portuguese Expeditionary Force swiftly marched to the Pyrenees front. At Ceret (26 Nov 1793), the allied army defeated the French but were unable to follow up their success. Despite these initial successes, the joint invading army failed to conquer Roussillon due to the news of the recapture of the port of Toulon, the army strength was reduced by over a half due to illness and the death of the Spanish commander on 13 March 1794.[48]

On 1 April 1794, the French Army of the Eastern Pyrenees under GdD Luc-Simion-August Dagobert attacked at Palau punching a 20km hole wide in the Allied centre and endangered the important fortress of Bellegarde. At the important heights of Vilar an Oms (28-29 Apr), the Spanish had initial success before their commander Conde de la Union overextended his line. The French attacked the centre and left on 30 April-1 May causing the Allies to withdraw into Spain. The

---

[45] Chartrand (1998) I: p4

[46] **Manuel de Godoy** (1767-1851) joined the *Guardias de Corps* in 1788 as a trooper which was the equivalent rank of 2nd Lieutenant in the regular army and was only open to the nobility. He soon came to the attention of the new King Carlos IV and especially his wife, María Luisa. By 1792, he had been promoted to the rank of Captain-General and appointed to the post of Minister of State. In March 1798, he fell out of favour only to be recalled in 1801 to command the forces dispatched against Portugal in the "War of the Oranges" and subsequently lead the much needed military reform. [Esdaile (1999) pp302-303]

[47] **General João (John) Forbes-Skelater** (1733-1808) was a British officer born in Aberdeenshire who transferred to reorganise assist in the reorganisation of the Portuguese Army under the Count of Lippe-Buckeburg in 1762. He was adjutant-general during the 1780s and promoted to general in 1789.

[48] Fuente (2011) p17-18

retreat descended into a rout with most of the ordnance lost when the civilian drivers absconded with their horses. Nevertheless, the Portuguese retired in good order.[49]

On 13 August 1794, the Allied Army attempted to relieve the fortress of Bellegarde. The Spanish were forced into another disordered retreat. On 19 November, the French decisively defeated the Spanish, dug in just north of Figueres, inflicting over 8,000 casualties and taking the Spanish fortress of Figueres (27 Nov 1794). With the imminent peace with France, General Gregorio de la Cuesta with 9,000 Spanish and 800 Portuguese infantry set out to attack the defences around Puig-Cerda.

On 22 July 1795 at Basel, Godoy negotiated the French withdrawal in exchange for the loss of the Island of Santo Domingo. He became known as the *Príncipe de la Paz* (Prince of the Peace).[50] On 26 July 1795, Cuesta led a frontal attack on the town of Puig-Cerda and 1,200 French were captured. The French at the neighbouring town of Belver were forced to surrender. It was not until 30 July, that the peace treaty was signed with France.

By the Treaty of San Ildefonso (19 Aug 1796), Spain became the ally of France and their combined naval power, compelled the Royal Navy to abandon the Mediterranean.[51] Negotiations for Portuguese neutrality collapsed when a Portuguese frigate brought news to the Royal Navy who destroyed the Franco-Spanish fleet off Cape St Vincent (14 Feb 1797).[52] Spain still hesitated to declare war on Portugal.

According to the Second Treaty of San Idelfonso (1 Oct 1800), Napoleon and her ally Spain demanded that Portugal enter into an alliance against Britain, open her ports to the French and Spanish shipping, and cede to Spain a major part of her national territory as security for the restoration of Trinidad, Mahon and Malta from occupation by the British. Portugal refused.

On 27 February 1801, Spain declared war on Portugal.

1802

Musician

1° and 2 ° **Miqueletes de Cataluña**
After Bueno

---

[49] Fuente (2011) p19-20
[50] Chartrand (1998) I: p5
[51] Taylor (2006) p87; Fuente (2011) p23.
[52] Fuente (2011) p23-24.

On 20 May 1801, a Spanish Army of 60,000 men under the command of Manuel de Godoy invaded Portugal in the north, centre and south. In the north, the Spanish were beaten and the Portuguese forces occupied Galician villages and towns. In the south, their tentative invasion of the Algarve was driven back into Spain. The only success was the immediate surrender of the frontier towns of Juromenha and Olivença garrisoned with Militia companies with French émigré commanders on 7 June. The regiments stationed there retired and join the main Portuguese army concentrated in Abrantes-Portalegre according to the usual Portuguese army strategy.

The towns of Elvas and Campo Maior refused to surrender. Godoy picked some oranges at nearby Elvas and sent these to the Queen of Spain with the message boasting that he would proceed to Lisbon. Thus, the conflict became better known as the "War of the Oranges." However, Godoy with his large army chose not to attack the main Portuguese group of fortresses around Elvas, the gateway to the open plains of the province of Alentejo or the main Portuguese army despite them being devoid of allies.

The only fighting occurred at Campo Maior where the Portuguese governor with its 1,200 garrison refused to surrender and was invested by the 8,000 Spanish force under General Negret started on 21 May.

On 28 May, with so little gains, the Spanish decided to accept negotiations fearing the intervention of the French Army Corps of General Lefebvre (Napoleon's brother-in-law) would enter the conflict. This corps had already entered Spain to "support" the Spanish Army of Godoy. These events caused the Spanish to think that a quick negotiation was required to protect their meagre territorial gains and exclude any French claims.

On 29 May, the 6,000 Spanish of D. Francisco Solano advanced towards Arronches where the outnumbered Portuguese force commanded by Colonel Carcome Lobo instead of withdrawing or fortifying the town decided to offer open battle. The Spanish cavalry outflanked the Portuguese resulting in their cavalry stampeding through their infantry and only the appearance of General Bernardim Freire de Andrade with 16 Portuguese battalions stabilised the situation. The Spanish chose to halt their pursuit fearing that this was the vanguard of a large army.

Peace negotiations were concluded on 6 June when the Prince Regent and future King John VI of Portugal signed the Treaty of Badajóz with the Spanish representative in which Olivença (renamed Olivenza) was ceded to Spain, an indemnity of £15 million paid and the ports closed to British ships. On 29 September 1801, the Treaty of Madrid upheld the tenets of the Peace of Badajóz with Portugal agreeing to pay a further £20 million to France.[53] The treaty incensed Napoleon because he had failed to overrun Portugal and bring her under French rule.

Following the peace of Amiens, in 1804, Spain was once again forced to become a French ally. Napoleon hoped that with the assistance of the Spanish Navy, he could gain control of the English Channel long enough to invade Britain.[54] This cost Spain her most of her navy at Trafalgar (18 Oct 1805) and consequently her overseas colonies.

On 24 May 1806, Godoy wrote to Napoleon that he wished to acquire a principality for himself in Portugal. However, on 27 June 1806 with the capture of Buenos Aires by the British roused strong feelings in Spain and forced Godoy to offer peace with Britain.[55] In an act of duplicity, on 5 October 1806, Godoy announced the mobilisation of the Spanish Army expecting Prussian victory. However, news of Napoleon's victory over Prussia caused Godoy to attempt to cover his nefarious plans by claiming that these troops were needed to attack Portugal.

Cazador dancing the Flamenco, c1807
By Henri Ganier-Tanconville, 1911

He sent the Emperor a number of expensive gifts including four of the finest Andalusian horses to replace the one that Napoleon had lost during his recent campaign.[56]

---

[53] Fuente (2011) pp24-26
[54] Oman (1902) I: p3
[55] Lefebvre (1969) pp13-14
[56] Otto von Pivka (1975) p4

Etruria Expeditionary Force 1806

One of the many complexities involved in the Franco-Spanish alliance was the Kingdom of Etruria. This had been created from the old Grand Duchy of Tuscany by the Treaty of Aranjuez (21 Mar 1801) between France and Spain as compensation for Ferdinand, the Bourbon Duke of Parma who relinquished claims to his territories in Northern Italy that had been occupied by France since 1796. His son Louis was named King of Etruria. The Grand Duke Ferdinand III of Tuscany received the secularized lands of the Archbishop of Salzburg.

In 1803, Louis I of Etruria (1773-1803) died and his younger son Charles Louis (1799-1883) succeeded him as Louis II. His mother María Luisa of Spain (1782-1824) was appointed regent. On 17 September 1805, French troops were withdrawn from the Kingdom of Etruria. To replace these troops, Spain agreed to send a division under General Don Gonzalo O'Farrell.[57] This force consisted of five battalions of infantry, one light infantry battalion, two cavalry regiments and an artillery company without cannon totalling 6,130 men (OOB 4).

OOB 4: Etruria Expeditionary Force of General O'Farrell.[58]
4,802 infantry, 1,258 cavalry and 100 gunners = 6,130 men

Infantry Brigade
I-III/*Rgto de Zamora* (Colonel Miguel Salcedo)	2,256 men

Infantry Brigade
I-II/ *Rgto de Guadalajara* (Col Vincente Martorell)	1,504 men
1° *Voluntarios de Cataluña* (Major Juan Francisco Víver)	1,042 men

Cavalry Brigade
Rgto de Caballería de Algarve (Colonel José de Yebra)	624 men, 406 horses
Rgto de Dragones de Villaviciosa (Col de Almanderez)	634 men, 393 horses

Artillery (Captain José López)
Artillería a Pie (Foot) Coy/4th Artillery Regt	100 men (no guns)

Captain Rafael de Llanza y de Valls[59] of the *Rgto de Guadalajara* recorded in his memoirs the 1329 km march from Spain to Italy in 62 days. This included 14 rest days. His diary recorded; Barcelona (3 Jan 1806), entered France at Le Boulou (10 Jan) before marching via Perpignan (11 Jan), Bezieres (16 Jan), Montpellier (20 Jan), Aix-en-Provence (29 Jan), Nice (9 Feb) crossing into Italy at San Remo (12 Feb)

---

[57] **Gonzalo O'Farrell** was born in Havana to a rich merchant, Don Juan José O'Farrell y Arriola (1721-79). In 1771, his father purchased him a commission in *Rgto de la Princessa*. He swiftly rose to Lt-Gen (1795), Inspector General of Infantry (1798), ambassador to Prussia (1799), honorary privy councillor (1805), Colonel General of the Artillery (1808) and Secretary of State for War (1808).
[58] Boppe (1899) p16-17
[59] **Rafael de Llanza y de Valls** was a captain of the *Regimiento de Guadalajara*. He was captured with his regiment in Denmark and "volunteered" to join the Joseph Napoleón Regiment that was recruited from Spanish prisoners of war. He later fought at Borodino before returning to Spain in 1813. He had by that time marched 33,083 km by his own reckoning. [Acosta (2009) pp67-121]

and finally arriving in Florence (5 Mar).[60] The Etruria Expeditionary Force of General O'Farrell garrisoned Livorno, Pisa and Florence in Etruria.

On 1 February 1807, the Etruria Expeditionary Force departed Florence to invade the Papal States and arrived in Rome before returning to Florence later in the month, a march of 60 *leguas* (334 km).[61] On 1 April 1807, it was decided that these Spanish troops would form the 2nd Spanish Division of the French *Corps d'Observation* stationed in Hanover (OOB 5). They took 80 days to march 1,831 km from Florence in Italy to Celle in Hanover: departed Florence (1 Apr), crossed the Apennines into the Kingdom of Italy (22 Apr), Italian Tyrol (2 May), the "Bavarian" Tyrol (8 May), Kingdom of Bavaria (17 May), Franconia (30 May), Hanover (10 June) and finally to Celle on 24 June 1807.[62]

On 10 December 1807, Etruria[63] was integrated into Metropolitan France and was split into three French *Départements* of Arno, Méditerranée and Ombrone. Louis II and his mother were promised the throne of the new Kingdom of Northern Lusitania by one of the clauses of the Treaty of Fontainebleau that set out the dismemberment of Portugal into three separate kingdoms. However, these intentions were destroyed by the French invasion of Spain in May 1808 (see Chapter 18).

Spanish cavalry and infantry awaiting departure
by Richard Knotel based upon the drawing of Christoph Suhr

---

[60] According to Captain Rafael de Llanza y de Valls, his regiment marched 97½ *leguas* (543 km) in January, 124 *leguas* (691 km) in February and 17 *leguas* (95 km) in the first days of March 1806. (1 *legua* = 20,000 *pies* = 5.573 km = 3.46 miles). The march was split into 3-4 day march stages of 12-22 *leguas* (67-123 km) each followed by a day of rest. The regiment averaged a respectable 28 km (17 miles) per day. [Acosta (2009) pp69-70 & 117]

[61] Acosta (2009) p70

[62] Acosta (2009) pp70-72 and Boppe (1899) p14

[63] In 1814, Tuscany was restored to its Habsburg Grand Dukes. In 1815, the Duchy of Lucca was carved out of Tuscany as a temporary compensation for the Bourbons of Parma until in 1847 when they could resume their rule over Parma.

Spanish Expeditionary Force 1807

As a French ally, on 5 February 1807, King Carlos IV of Spain agreed to send a corps of 14,000 under Spain's most capable general, Marquis de la Romana to Northern Germany. On 19 February 1807, Spain joined the Continental Blockade against Britain. The *División del Norte* (Division of the North) consisted of four infantry regiments (12 Bns), five cavalry regiments, and two light infantry battalions with supporting artillery and engineers.

OOB 5: *División del Norte* in March 1807[64]
6,632 infantry, 1,620 cavalry and 427 gunners = 8,679 men

Infantry Brigade	
I-III/22° *Rgto de Asturias* (Col. Luís Dellevielleuze)	2,282 men
1° *Voluntarios de Barcelona* (Major José Borrelas)	1,240 men
Infantry Brigade	
I-III/27° *Rgto de la Princesa* (Col. Conde de San Román)	2,332 men
III/10° *Rgto de Guadalajara*	778 men
Cavalry Brigade	
1° *Rgto de Caballería del Rey* (Colonel Miguel Gambra)	540 men
4° *Rgto del Infante* (Colonel Francisco Maríano)	540 men
3° *Rgto de Dragones de Almansa* (Col Juan A. Caballero)	540 men
Artillery (Brigadier Ignácio Martinez Vallejo)	
Artillería a Pie (foot artillery) Company/3rd Artillery Regt	270 men
Artillería a Caballo (horse artillery) Coy/3rd Artillery Regt	89 men
Train Company	68 men

La Romana's Division was placed under the command of Marshal Brune, garrisoning Hamburg and Lübeck. On 3 July 1807, King Gustav IV Adolf of Sweden renounced a truce with France. Marshal Brune had two French Divisions of GdD Boudet and GdD Molitor (16,485 infantry and 405 gunners) and the Dutch Divisions of GdD Dumonceau and GdD Bertrand supported by GdD Bertrand's Cavalry Brigade (13,856 infantry, 729 gunners, 1,112 troopers).[65] On 6 July 1807, La Romana's two divisions force-marched 482 km in 18 days to join Brune in Swedish Pomerania.[66]

On 24 July, Marshal Brune was able to reoccupy the siege lines around Stralsund after defeating the Swedish Army along the Peene River. He was later reinforced by the Kingdom of Italy Division of GdD Domenico Pino (8 Bns, 8 Sq), the Baden Contingent (6 Bns, 1 Sq) plus the I-II/Würzburg IR, I-II/1st Berg IR and II-IV/Nassau IR that had participated in the failed siege of Kolberg. On 6 August, the *1° Voluntarios de Cataluña* supported by the *Dragones de Villaviciosa* repulsed a Swedish attempt to relieve the siege. On 18 August, the Spanish contingent marched 301 km to Bergdorf and arrived in the Kingdom of Hanover on the 24th.[67] On 20 August,

---

64 Boppe (1899) p15
65 Smith (1998) p253
66 Averaged 30 km per day. [Acosta (2009) 72]
67 Acosta (2009) p73

the 15,000 Swedish defenders spiked their 500 cannons in the fortress, burned their gun carriages and evacuated Stralsund for the Island of Rügen. Stralsund was handed over to the French on 24 August and Rügen on 7 September 1807.

OOB 6: French *Légion d'Honneur* awarded to Spanish officers for the Siege of Stralsund[68]

Commander
    Major General Kindelan, *Chef* of the *Rgto de Ultonia*
Staff
    Col. Caballero of *Rgto de Dragones de Almansa* and Chief of Staff was promoted to Brigadier, Lt Kindelan of the *Rgto de Ultonia* was ADC to his father, General Kindelan and was also promoted to Captain.
7° Rgto de Zamora
    Brigadier Salcedo
10° Rgto de Guadalajara
    Colonel Montorell
Artillery
    Captain Pómar commanded the defence of Redoubt No. 6 against the fire from Swedish gunners.

For the action of 6 August 1807.

1° Voluntarios de Cataluña
    Captains Porta, Blanco, Vila and Senespleda. 1st Lt Camilleri to Captain, 2nd Lt Montros and Pineyro to 1st Lt.
5° Rgto de Dragones de Villaviciosa
    Captain del Rio was promoted to Colonel, Captains D'Aranda and Rute were also promoted to Lt-Col, 2nd Lt Contreras was promoted to 1st Lt.

OOB 7: Staff of La Romana's Spanish Expeditionary Force (Nov 1807)[69]
10,669 infantry, 3,291 cavalry, 390 gunners and 108 sappers = 14,457 men

Commander	Lieutenant-General Marquis de La Romana.[70]
Second in Command	Major General Juan Kindelan.[71]
Aides-de-Camp	Col. Marquis de Crèvecoeur, Col. Juan Caro.
	Col. Pedro de los Ríos, Captain Agustino de Llano.
	Captain Francisco Xavier Riera and Captain Julio O'Neill.
Chief of Staff	Brigadier José Montes Salazar.
Staff Officers	Col. Ignacio Martinez Vallejo, Col. Maríano Reugel, Col. Juan António Caballero, Major José O'Donnell, Captain Juan de la Vera and Captain Pedro Guerrero.
Secretaries	Captain Estamilas Captain Sandrez Salvador and Captain Juan Ricardo.

---

[68] Boppe (1899) pp26-27
[69] Boppe (1899) p15
[70] He was considered to be a pro-British general with unquestioned loyalty to the King and Godoy.
[71] The pro-French General Kindelan replaced the former commander of the Etruria Expeditionary Force, General O'Farrell, as second in command.

OOB 8: La Romana's Spanish Expeditionary Force (Nov 1807)[72]

1st Division (Colonel Dellavielleuze) in Hamburg
Infantry Brigade
I-III/*22° Rgto de Asturias* (Col. Luís Silvela y de Le Vielleuze)	2176 men
1° Voluntarios de Barcelona (Major José Borrelas)	1313 men

Infantry Brigade
I-III/*27° Rgto de la Princesa* (Col. Conde de San Román)	2016 men

Cavalry Brigade
1° Rgto de Caballería del Rey (Colonel Miguel Gambra)	671 men/551 horses
4° Rgto del Infante (Col Francisco Maríano)	682 men/593 horses

2nd Division (Colonel de Salcedo) in Lübeck
Infantry Brigade
I-III/*7° Rgto de Zamora* (Col Miguel Salcedo)	1973 men

Infantry Brigade
I-III/*10° Rgto de Guadalajara* (Col Vincente Martorell)	2021 men
1° Voluntarios de Cataluña (Major Jun Francisco Víver)	1170 men

Cavalry Brigade
9° Rgto de Caballería de Algarve (Col José de Yebra)	646 men/539 horses
3° Rgto de Dragones de Almansa (Col J. A. Caballero)	633 men/575 horses
5° Rgto de Dragones de Villaviciosa (Col Almanderez)	659 men/558 horses

Artillery (Lt-Col. Breson)
3° *Artillería a Pie* Coy/3rd Artillery Regt (Captain Lamor)	223 men
1° (*Artillería a Caballo*) Coy/3rd Artillery Regt (Capt Lopez)	99 men/72 horses
Train Company	68 men/292 horses

Engineers (Brigadier Hermozilla, Inspector General Las Heras)
Sappers	108 men

Romana's Infantry on the March
By Richard Knötel after Christoph Suhr

---

[72] Boppe (1899) p15

La Romana in Denmark 1808

On 31 July 1807, Denmark was forced to accept the Continental Blockade. In response, Britain invaded Denmark on 16 August and on 7 September after the bombardment of Copenhagen, Denmark surrendered, and her fleet taken to Britain. On 30 October 1807, Denmark signed an alliance with France. In February 1808, Denmark declared war on Great Britain. The Spanish with French, Dutch and Belgian troops formed Marshal Brune's 45,000 strong Observation Corps sent to garrison the Danish coast against invasion and possibly take part in the operations against Sweden.

OOB 9: The Spanish contingent of Brune's Observation Corps (Mar 1808)[73]

10,667 infantry, 3,047 cavalry, 477 gunners and 127 sappers = 14,318 men

Spanish Corps (Marquis de la Romana)
    Artillery Commander (Col J. Martmez-Vallego)

1st (La Romana) Division
Infantry Brigade
    I-III/Rgto de Asturias (Col. Luís Silvela y de Le Vielleuze)   2,103 men
    I/Voluntarios de Barcelona (Major J. F. Víver)   1,266 men
Infantry Brigade
    I-III/Rgto de la Princesa (Col. Conde de San Román)   1,969 men
Cavalry Brigade
    Rgto de Caballería del Rey   634 men, 615 horses
    Rgto de Caballería del Infante   615 men, 599 horses
    Rgto de Dragones de Almansa   598 men, 566 horses
Artillery
    3° Artillería a Pie Coy/3rd Artillery Regt (6x 8-pdrs+2 How)
    1° Artillería a Caballo Coy/3rd Artillery Regt (6x 4-pdrs)   240 men
         One Engineer Company   127 men

2nd (Kindelan) Spanish Division
Infantry Brigade
    I-III/Rgto de Zamora (Col. M. Salcedo)   2,096 men
    II/Voluntarios de Cataluña (Major J. F. Víver)   1,164 men
Infantry Brigade
    I-III/Rgto de Guadalajara   2,069 men
Cavalry Brigade (Col. J. d'Yebra)
    Rgto de Caballería de Algarve (Col. J. d'Yebra)   572 men, 522 horses
    Rgto de Dragones de Villaviciosa   628 men, 531 horses
Artillery
    Artillería a Pie coy/4th Artillery Regt (6x 4-pdrs+2 6.4in How)
    Artillería a Pie coy/4th Artillery Regt (4x 4-pdrs+2 6.4in How)
                                      237 men

---

[73] Oman (1902) I: pp607-11 and Godcot (1924)

The *Regimientos de Guadalajara* and *de Asturias* garrisoned the Island of Zealand near the royal residence of Roskilde and the Spanish troops were surrounded by the main Danish Army of Observation. On 31 July 1808, *Regimientos de Guadalajara* and *de Asturias* mutinied at Roskilde when instructed to take the oath to King Joseph Bonaparte of Spain, killing the ADC to General Fririon and threatening to march on Copenhagen. The next day Danish troops disarmed both regiments were put under guard in various points in the island. Only 150 men from both regiments were able to escape.[74]

Spanish troops on the march with their families
[After Suhr by Richard Knotel]

The Cataluña and Barcelona Light Infantry Battalions were the more exotic units of the Spanish Army. They provided a splash of colour and élan amongst the two Spanish Divisions in Denmark. They had the additional honour of escaping the clutches of the French and fighting under Blake's Army in Galicia. By stripping the equipment from the other artillery companies, four fully equipped artillery companies arrived in Denmark in 1807, one of which was horse artillery (*artillería a caballo*).

---

[74] Oman (1902) p373

OOB 10: The French and Dutch contingents of Brune's Corps in Feb 1808[75]
French: 14,783 infantry, no cavalry, 413 gunners = 14,318 men
Dutch: 13,836 infantry, 1,112 cavalry and 94 gunners = 15,142 men

1st Division (GdD Boudet)
Fririon Brigade

I-II/*3e Légère*	1,670 men

Valory Brigade

I-III/*56e Ligne*	2,664 men
I-III/*93e Ligne*	1,737 men
Artillery	208 men

2nd Division (GdD Molitor)
Leguay Brigade

I-III/*2e Ligne*	2,178 men
I-III/*16e Ligne*	2,462 men

Castella Brigade

I-III/*37e Ligne*	2,078 men
I-III/*67e Ligne*	1,994 men
Artillery	205 men

Dumonceau (Dutch) Division (From 8e Corps)
Van Helkdring Brigade

I-III/*3e* Dutch *Chasseurs à Pied*	2,491 men
I-III/*3e* Dutch *Ligne*	2,096 men
I-II/*4e* Dutch *Ligne*	1,637 men

Gras Brigade

I-II/*6e* Dutch *Ligne*	1,737 men
I-II/*9e* Dutch *Ligne*	1,943 men

Gratien Brigade

I-II/*2e* Dutch *Chasseurs à Pied*	1,316 men
I-II/*7e* Dutch *Ligne*	1,086 men
I-II/*8e* Dutch *Ligne*	1,530 men

Carteret Cavalry Brigade

I-IV/*3e* Dutch *Hussards*	568 men
I-III/*Duke of Arenberg Belgian Chevau-légers*	450 men
Imperial *Gendarmes*	94 men
Artillery	94 men

On 11 June 1808 some Spanish officers arrived in London to ask for British help to enable the Division to escape from the French and return to Spain. A British agent called Robertson who was an Irish Catholic priest was dispatched to make contact with La Romana.

On 24 June, three Spanish officers who were eye-witnesses of the Spanish revolt arrived at La Romana's headquarters, conveyed by the Royal Navy. La Romana was finally convinced that there was open war in Spain between France and Spain. His

---

[75] Boppe (1899) p21 and Gofcot (1824)

problem was that his force was so far from home. He trusted the planning to José Guerrero, Joaquín Lamor, Pablo Ventades and Manuel Zacarés of the Artillery. It was decided that the return by sea would be less dangerous than a long march over land. The British Government agreed to dispatch the Royal Navy to embark the Spanish.

Guerrero of the artillery was entrusted with observing the movements of Marshal Bernadotte's Corps in Northern Germany but unfortunately he was captured. Even under torture for about a month, he did not divulge the Spanish plans.[76] Manuel Zacarés of the Artillery was also captured.[77]

Meanwhile, Napoleon had ordered a series of thrusts outward from Madrid in an attempt to subdue Spain. On 19 July, GdD Dupont was trapped at Bailén by three Spanish Divisions and was forced to surrender his Corps after a valiant fight. This gave great impetus to the Spanish cause and that of subjugated Europe and encouraged the British to intervene.

Spanish Grenadiers and Sappers on Parade
After Christoph Suhr by Richard Knotel

---

76 **José Guerrero** was finally interned in France and in 1812 he managed to escape back to Spain where he fought with distinction.

77 In 1811, **Manuel Zacarés** escaped from the prisoner of war camp in France and reached Russian lines. In Russia, he assisted the Russian engineer GM Agustín de Betancourt y Molina (1758-1824), another native of Spain, during the winter campaign in Moscow and was given command of part of the Russian vanguard artillery. He later was commander of a Don Cossack Horse Artillery Battery and on 16 Feb 1814 directed the Russian artillery in the storming of Nemours defended by a depot battalion of the Imperial Guard. He returned to Spain in 1815.

OOB 11: Spanish Garrisons in Denmark in May 1808[78]

Jutland Division (General Kindelan)
Garrisoned the small towns of Fredericia, Aarhus and Randers in southern Jutland were mixed with Dutch Light Cavalry and Danish Infantry.

Spanish Garrison

I-III/7° *Rgto de Zamora*	Viele, Fredericia & Kolding
1ˢᵗ *Rgto de Caballería del Rey*	Horsens, Skanderborg & Aarhuus
4° *Rgto de Caballería del Infante*	Randers & Maríager
9° *Rgto de Caballería de Algarve*	Tonder, Husum & Tonning

Carteret Dutch Cavalry Brigade
3e Dutch *Hussards*
Duke of Arenberg Belgian *Chevau-légers*

Danish Infantry

Garrison of Langelan Island (Lt-Col Gauthier of the 37e *Ligne*)
1° *Voluntarios de Cataluña*
800 Danish Infantry
A company of French Grenadiers from 37e Ligne

Garrison of Island of Zealand (GdB Fririon)
The main Danish Army of Observation surrounded the old royal residence of Roskilde.
I-III/10° *Rgto de Guadalajara*
I-III/22° *Rgto de Asturias*

Nybourg Division (General de La Romana)
The garrison of Fünen was commanded by La Romana with his headquarters at Nyberg. The 4,500 Spanish were split into detachments throughout Fünen Island separated by the 3,000 Danish garrison of Odense.

I/27° *Rgto de la Princesa*	Nyborg & Kjerteminde
II/27° *Rgto de la Princesa*	Assens
I/27° *Rgto de la Princesa*	Middlefart
1° *Voluntarios de Barcelona*	Svendborg
3° *Rgto de Dragones de Almansa*	Odense & Bogense
5° *Rgto de Dragones de Villaviciosa*	Faaborg
Artillery and Engineers	Nyborg & Kjertemunde

Depot in Hamburg (Brigadier Hermosillas)

Depot (500 men)	Hamburg & Altona

---

[78] Boppe (1899) pp44-5

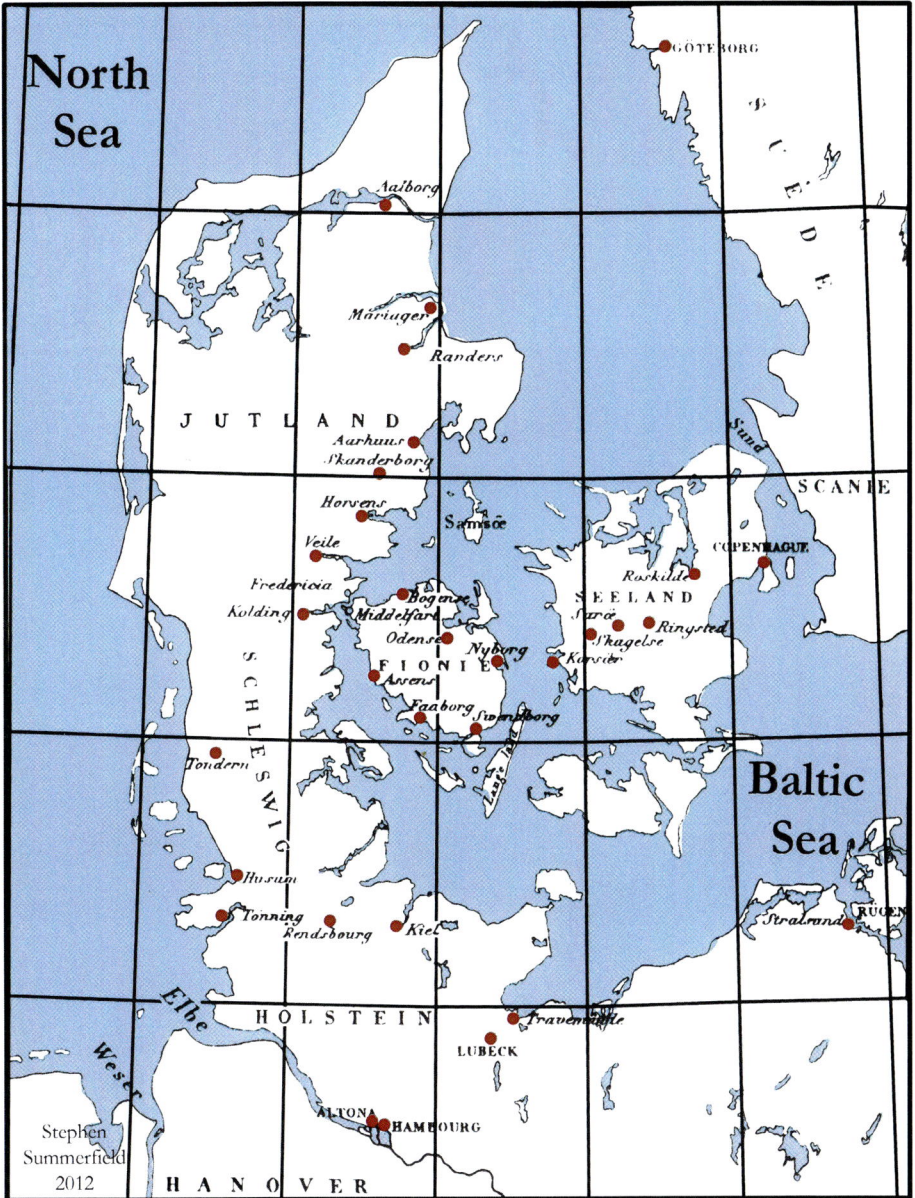

Map of Denmark in 1808

Stephen
Summerfield
2012

On 22 July 1808, Marshal Bernadotte sent La Romana a letter that instructed his men to pledge an oath of loyalty to King Joseph Bonaparte of Spain. La Romana replied that he feared his men would mutiny. He needed time to gather his widely dispersed command from Jutland, Fionia Island and Zeeland. He ordered his division to concentrate on the Danish Island of Nyberg. French and Danish troops suppressed a Spanish mutiny in Zeeland capturing the *Regimiento de Asturias* and *de Guadalajara*.

Spanish Infantry playing cards
By Richard Knötel after Christoph Suhr

The *Algarve* Cavalry Regiment being furthest from Nyberg surrendered without a fight and two of their officers betrayed the scheme to the French. The 3,500 soldiers were prisoners were dispersed to a number of different camps in France including the two regiments that had already been captured and disarmed. On 13 February 1809, many of these captives "volunteered" to join the Regiment Joseph Napoléon in French Service commanded by GdD Jean Kindelan (1759-1822).[79]

On 27 August 1808, the Royal Naval squadron of Admiral Sir Richard Keat seized the Danish port of Nyberg and embarked 9,000 Spanish troops concentrated there. Lamor and Ventades of the artillery were able to embark twenty-five pieces of artillery that had been brought from Spain in British ships.

---

[79] von Pivka (1978) 10 and Dempsey (2002) pp260-1

OOB 12: Units evacuated by the Royal Navy on 27 August 1808[80]

Infantry
I-III/*Rgto de la Princesa*	56/1,953
I-III/*Rgto de Zamora*	39/1,757
Detachment/*Rgto de Guadalajara*	2/120
Detachment/*Rgto de Asturias*	2/20
Other ill personnel	0/200

Light Infantry
1° Cazadores de Cataluña Bn.	42/1,066
1° Cazadores de Barcelona Bn.	37/1,205

Dragoons without their horses
I-IV/ *Rgto de Dragones de Almansa*	38/560
I-IV/ *Rgto de Dragones de Villaviciosa*	32/580

Heavy Cavalry without their horses
I-IV/*Rgto de Caballería del Infante*	34/561
I-IV/*Rgto de Caballería del Rey*	38/560
Detachment/*Rgto de Caballería de Algarve*	1/12

Technical Troops
Sapper Company	5/59
Artillery (13x4-pdrs, 6x 8-pdrs & 6x 6.4in How)	14/349

Cazador, fusilier and officer of Romana's Division, 1807
By an unknown German artist.

---

[80] The unit strengths are for 9 October 1808 when they returned to Spain [Brum (1822)]

The Marquis de la Romana

General Pedro Caro y Sureda, 3rd Marquis de la Romana was born at Palma de Mallorca in the Balearic Islands on 2 October 1761. When his father died, King Carlos III appointed the two brothers as Royal Naval Cadets on 7 July 1775. Pedro studied Hebrew and mathematics at Salamanca University, and afterwards, humanities and arts at the Seminario de Nobles in Madrid. He was commissioned in 1778 into the Spanish Navy.

In 1783, he participated in the reconquest of Minorca from the British. In the final months of the war, he was assigned to the blockade of Gibraltar. After the war, he retired to private life in Valencia where he amassed one of the largest private libraries in Spain.

Pedro Caro y Sureda, III
Marqués de la Romana (1761-1811)
Portrait by Vicente Lopez Y Portaña

In 1793, he entered the army as colonel of light cavalry at the start of the War of the First Coalition against the French. By 1795, he had risen to the rank of Lieutenant-General (*Teniente General*) and once again retired upon conclusion of hostilities. In 1802, he was appointed Captain-General of Catalonia. In 1805, he was assigned to the High War Council as General Director of the Engineer Corps.

In 1807, he was chosen to lead the *División del Norte* that performed garrison duties in Hamburg and later Denmark under Marshal Bernadotte. Upon hearing of the insurrection against the French, La Romana arranged the evacuation of 9,000 of the 15,000 Spanish by the Royal Navy on 27 August back to Spain.

La Romana arrived at Santander and was appointed commander of the Army of the Left on 11 November, which as fate would have it, was destroyed in battle the day before under the command of General Blake. On 26 November, La Romana assumed effective command of the remaining army of 6,000 men including the remnants of his soldiers whom he had extricated from Denmark.

La Romana supported Sir John Moore's retreat from Salamanca to León and then to Galicia. Moore wrote many letters to La Romana demanding closer co-operation of the Spanish forces with his own. The Spanish troops fought a number of rearguard actions to delay the French advance. On 26 December Sir John Moore abandoned La Romana at Benavente to head north to La Coruña. Without British support, his army retreated westwards into Galicia by the most difficult and direct way.

On 9 January 1809, he reached Valdeorras, where he supported the revolt against the French in Galicia. La Romana continued to act in support of the Portuguese in an attempt to prevent the second French invasion of Portugal by Soult in February and March 1809. Following the French defeat at Puente San Payo on 6 June 1809, Marshal Soult abandoned his attempts to re-establish French rule in Galicia and when Soult moved against the British on the Portuguese frontier, La Romana drove the French from Asturias before retiring with 8,000 men behind the Lines of Torres Vedra.

On 24 August 1809, he resigned the command of the Army when he was appointed a member of the Central Junta. In 1810, he returned to military operations under Wellington but died suddenly on 23 January 1811 of natural causes while preparing the relief of Badajóz. At news of his death, Wellington wrote, "his loss is the greatest which the cause could sustain."

El juramento de las tropas del Marqués de la Romana
Manuel Castellano, 1850

Spanish Line Infantrymen

Left is the a fusilier id *Rgto de Zaragoza* and right is a fusilier smoking a
cigarette from the *Rgto de Guadaljara* in M1805 uniform.

By Bradford, 1809

Chapter 3
Line Infantry

In 1788, Carlos IV inherited 27 Spanish Line Infantry Regiments with a complement of 2,669 officers and 66,702 men.[81] Each regiment with two battalions each of one grenadier (*Granaderos*) and four fusilier companies. The fusilier company had 160 men and the grenadier company had 120 men. The grenadiers from two regiments were used to form converged grenadier battalions as in the Prussian Army of Frederick II. Due to the need to save money, the regulation dated 21 June 1791 permitted the rapid demobilisation in peacetime by reducing the number of men in each company by half.[82]

By 1792, the Spanish army comprised a total of 38 regiments. Godoy effectively ruled Spain as the Captain-General of the Army and *Duque de la Alcudia* allocated these 38 infantry regiments into nine Permanent Brigades including the 1st & 2nd (Guard) Brigades. (See OOB 13).

OOB 13: The nine Permanent Infantry Brigades[83]

1st (Guard) Brigade: *Guardias Españoles*	Joaquín Palafox
2nd (Guard) Brigade: *Guardias Valonas*	Pedro Fort de St. Martin
3rd (*Granaderos y Cazadores*) Brigade *Granaderos* and *Cazadores*	Eugenio Nero
4th Brigade: *Reina, Burgos, Mallorca, Málaga*	Pedro Rodríguez de la Burria
5th Brigade: *Príncipe, Granada, Valencia*	Francisco Xavier Negrete
6th Brigade: *Saboya, Sevilla, Extremadura*	Rafael Basco
7th Brigade: *Soria, Murcia, Navarra*	Valentín Belvis de Moncada y Pizam
8th Brigade: *Córdoba, Iberia*	Joaquín de Oquenco
9th Brigade: *1º de Cataluña, Tarragona, Gerona*	Juan M. Vives

On 26 August 1802, Godoy introduced new regulations for the infantry that confirmed the existence of the depot battalion in each regiment. Each of the thirty-five Spanish and four foreign regiments had two field battalions and a depot

---

[81] Between 1789 -91, three of the regiments were renamed [Esdaile (1988) p201].

[82] Nafziger (1992) p15

[83] Nafziger (1993) p6

battalion.[84] In addition, the field battalions were re-organised: the I battalion had two grenadier companies and two fusilier companies (*blanquillos*). The II and III (depot) battalion had four companies of fusiliers.

The peacetime establishment was:

I Battalion Staff
1 *coronel* (colonel), 1 *sargento mayor* (major), 1 *ayudante mayor* (adjutant major), 1 *capellán* (chaplain), 1 *cirujano* (surgeon), 1 *armero* (armourer), 1 *tambor mayor* (drum-major).

II Battalion Staff
1 *teniente coronel* (lt-col), 1 *ayudante mayor* (adjutant major), 1 *abanderado* (standard-bearer), 1 *capellán* (chaplain), 1 *cirujano* (surgeon), 1 *armero* (armourer).

III (Depot) Battalion Staff
1 *comandante* (commandant), 1 *ayudante mayor* (adjutant major), 1 *abanderado* (standard-bearer), 1 *capellán* (chaplain), 1 *cirujano* (surgeon), 1 *armero* (armourer).

Fusilier Company (87 men)
1 *capitán* (captain), *teniente* (1st lt), *subteniente* (2nd lt), *sargento primero* (first sergeant), 4 *sargentos segundos* (second sergeants), 4 *tambores* (drummers), 8 *cabos primeros* (corporals), 8 *cabos segundos* (lance corporals), 60 soldiers.

The total strength of a regiment was 19 staff, 70 company officers and 1,008 other ranks.[85] In practice it was much less, for example the company of Lieutenant Ruiz on 2 May 1808 had only 35 men. At time of war, the companies were increased.

I Battalion Staff (21 men)
1 *coronel* (colonel), 1 *teniente coronel* (lt-col), 1 *sargento mayor* (major), 1 *cadete* (cadet), 2 *tenientes* (1st lts), 1 *capellán* (chaplain), 1 clerk, 1 *cirujano* (surgeon), 1 *tambor mayor* (drum-major), 2 *pífanos* (fifers), 1 *cabo de zapadores* (sapper corporal), 6 *zapadores* (sappers), 1 *armero* (armourer), 1 *preboste* (provost).

II Battalion Staff (16 men)
1 *teniente coronel* (lt-col), 1 *ayudante* (adjutant), 1 *cadete* (cadet), 1 *capellán* (chaplain), 1 *cirujano* (surgeon), 2 *pífanos* (fifers), 1 *cabo de zapadores* (sapper corporal),
6 *zapadores* (sappers), 1 *armero* (armourer), 1 *preboste* (provost).

III (Depot) Battalion Staff (16 men)
1 *comandante* (commandant), 1 *ayudante mayor* (adjutant major), 1 *cadete* (cadet), 1 *capellán* (chaplain), 1 *cirujano* (surgeon), 2 *pífanos* (fifers), 1 *cabo de zapadores* (sapper corporal), 6 *zapadores* (sappers), 1 *armero* (armourer), 1 *preboste* (provost).

Grenadier Company (112 men)
1 *capitán* (captain), 1 *teniente* (1st lt), 1 *subteniente* (2nd lt), 1 *sargento primero* (first sergeant), 2 *sargentos segundos* (second sergeants), 4 *cabos primeros* (corporals), 4 *cabos segundos* (lance corporals), 2 *tambores* (drummers), 96 *granaderos* (grenadiers).

---

[84] Esdaile (1988) p7
[85] Sanudo (1999) p160

Fusilier Company (206 men)

1 *capitán primero* (1st captain), 1 *capitán segundo* (2nd captain), 2 *teniente* (1st lt), 2 *subteniente* (2nd lt), 1 *sargento primero* (first sergeant), 5 *sargentos segundos* (second sergeants), 8 *cabos primeros* (corporals), 8 *cabos segundos* (lance corporals), 4 *tambores* (drummers), 174 *fusileros* (fusiliers).

Each company had eight *tiradores* (skirmishers) which equated to 32 *tiradores* per battalion. Their task was to advance 100-200m in front of the battalion to prevent their opponents from encroaching within musket range. Against the French, this meant that the Spanish had barely a third or a quarter of the skirmishers who were commanded by their own officers and NCOs.

It is interesting to note that it was common for Spanish Infantry to serve as Marines on board ships. On 19 October 1805, there were 6,881 naval personnel, 4,135 infantry and 931 gunners from the marine artillery serving on board the fifteen Spanish ships that fought at Trafalgar. The Regiments included *Regimientos de África,*

Spanish Infantry Officers
Augsburger, 1807

de Córdoba, de la Corona and *de Soria.* There were also detachments from *Regimiento de América* and the *2° Cazadores de Cataluña.* Each infantry regiment supplied 2-3 companies. The percentage of soldiers at 42% of a total ship's company was almost double that used by the French (28%) and Royal Navy (15%).[86] It is probable that these regiments were still wearing their M1802 uniforms.

---

[86] Adkin (2005) pp305-306, quoting Gravina's report dated 19 October 1805.

Infantry Drill

Spanish Infantry on Parade, 1807

Between 1788 and 1801, the Spanish army used a version of the Prussian drill developed by Frederick the Great. In 1803, the Spanish officially adopted the French Regulations of 1791 and in general, the Army attempted to follow contemporary French tactics.

However, the training and the drill was often specific to the regiment where different words of command were used and the method of loading a musket varied. The inadequacies of these variations was very clearly shown in the Getafe exercises of 1808 near Madrid, where General Blake failed in his attempt to get the infantry to follow the practice in his own regiment of loading the musket on the right side rather than the left side. Elsewhere the Swiss Colonel Taxler found his troops unfit because they had not left their garrison for eight years.[87]

Spanish Grenadiers on Parade
By Richard Knötel after Christoph Suhr

---

[87] Sanuda (1999) 149 and Nafziger (1992) p24

Infantry Flags

For an in-depth study the reader should start with Luís Sorando Muzás of the Spanish Army Museum.[88] The pattern of flags was changed in 1728, when Philip V issued a Royal Ordnance specifying the following:

> "...*Each battalion of our troops is to have three flags 11* pies *high (230cm) each pole including a 12 inch ferrule and spearhead.* Coronela *flag will be white with the Royal coat of arms and the others, white with the Cross of Burgundy. At the corners of each one there will be the arms of the kingdom or province the Regiment takes its name from, or particular devices due to custom and seniority...*"

Each battalion had three M1728 flags measuring 230cm square and the flagstaff 357cm. This pattern lasted without significant changes until 1843 when the red-yellow-red colours replaced the royal arms *Coronela* flag.

With the accession of the new monarch in 1760, Carlos III, the royal coat of arms no longer had the red Cross of Burgundy. The Royal Ordnance of 1762 stipulated that the flag dimensions were reduced to 146cm square on an 8.5 *pies* (237cm) flagstaff. The flagstaff was lined with crimson, green or blue velvet with metal gallon and spiral studding in the button colour. The finial was in the shape of an inverted heart. Both sides of the flag were the same.

The number of flags per battalion was reduced from three to two flags. The I Bn carried one *Coronela* and one *Sencilla* flag. The II Bn carried two *Sencilla* flags.

The **M1762 *Coronela***[89] had a very large Royal coat of arms surrounded by an ornate chain. In the corners were the provincial coat of arms surmounted by the ducal crown except for *Regimientos de la Reina* who used the Royal crown. The shields were surrounded by a yellow frame with four flags and two cannon barrels.

The **M1762 *Sencilla***[90] had the coat of arms of the kingdoms or provinces on the four tips of the red Cross of Burgundy.

In 1762, the infantry immediately reduced the number of their flags by withdrawing from service and destroying the surplus *Sencillas*. The new M1762 pattern was adopted slowly. For example, the *Regimiento de Mallorca* still used their M1728 flags awarded in 1749 until at least 1783. A *Coronela* cost 1,160 *reales* and the less ornate *Sencilla* cost 890 *reales*. Initially, the flags were renewed every two and half years but in 1773 this was changed to every ten years and confirmed on 20 April 1784. By

---

[88] The book is 206 pages long with a CD of about 1,200 colour photos of flags and 700 pages of text describing the flags and history [Luís Sorando Muzás (2001) *Banderas, estandartes y trofeos del Museo del Ejército 1700-1843, Catálogo razonado*, Spanish Minstry of Defence.]

[89] The *Coronela* was equivalent to the Colonel's Colour in the British Army and was carried by I Bn.

[90] The *Sencilla* (also known as *Ordenanza*) was the Regimental flag and was carried by all battalions until 1802 when reduced one flag per battalion, it was carried by the II-III Bns while the I Bn carried the *Coronela*.

about 1790, all the regiments used the M1762 pattern and when in 1791 the infantry regiments formed III Bns, these received two *Sencillas*.

Most of the 70 flags and standards used in the War of the First Coalition (1792-95) against the French were replaced due to battle damage or loss to the enemy with new M1762 pattern flags. Some regiments received battle honours on their flags on the *Coronela* below the Royal coat of arms and at the intersection of the Cross of Burgundy on the *Sencilla*.[91] The battle honours for the retreat from Irún (1 Aug 1794) were awarded to the *Irlandés de Ultonia*, the *Suizo de Reding*[92] and the *Provincial de Tuy*.[93] For the battle of Colledo de Ollarregiu (24 July 1795) the I/II/*Regimiento de África* was rewarded.[94]

The Royal Ordnance of 26 August 1802 reduced the number of flags to one per battalion so each three battalion infantry regiment had one *Coronela* and two *Sencillas*. These surplus flags should have been destroyed but many were laid up in churches[95] and many of these were re-used during the Peninsular War.[96]

During the Peninsular War (1808-14), practically all Regiments had to renew their flags whether lost in combat or battle damaged. No new regulations were published so they conformed to the M1762 pattern. However, in about 1812 when all the infantry regiments were reduced to a single battalion which by the regulations should only carry the *Coronela*, there appeared the M1812 pattern with the royal coat of arms and the Cross of Burgundy. This symbolized the merger of the *Coronela* and *Sencilla* flags. These M1812 flags including *Regimiento de la Princesa* and *2° Voluntarios de Barcelona* had the Spanish coat of arms in the centre of the Cross of Burgundy. This pattern co-existed with the M1762 pattern and there were many variations.[97]

The new battalions and regiments adopted flags of very diverse designs often re-using those that had been deposited in churches. Most flags had a white field but also those with black, crimson and yellow fields were used.

---

[91] Sorando Muzás (2000) p56
[92] Flag of *Regimiento de Tuy* (1815-44: Reg. No. 21161) [Sorando Muzás (2000) p157].
[93] Flag of *Suizo de Reding* is Registry No. 21285 [Sorando Muzás (2000) p157].
[94] Alas the flag of the *Regimiento de África* was destroyed in a fire at the Royal Arsenal in 1882. [Note 1956 in Sorando Muzás (2000) p157]
[95] *Regimientos de Barbastro* (1794-1811: Reg. No. 21305), *Baza* (1808-15: Reg. No. 40838) and *Candas* (1808-12: Reg. No. 21160). [Note 202 in Sorando Muzás (2000) p157].
[96] Sorando Muzás (2000) pp56-57
[97] Sorando Muzás (2000) p56

Line Infantry Regiments
Rgto de África (Est. 1559)

Tercio Fijo de Sicilia was formed on 23 October 1559 by Don Jerónimo de Mendoza, Viceroy of Naples. On 10 February 1718, *Rgto Fijo de Sicilia* became *Rgto de África*. Absorbed *Rgto de Almansa* (Est. 28 Sept 1808) on 2 March 1815.

Campaign History: The regiment was distinguished in the Roussillon campaign including at Egui and Ollaregui (1795). Detachments acted as Marines on Spanish Naval ships at Trafalgar (21 Oct 1805). In May 1808, I & III Bns were in Port of Algeciras on the Bay of Gibraltar (*Bahía de Algeciras*); II Bn was in Port of San Sebastián in northern Spain on the coast of the Bay of Biscay just 20 km from the French border (898 men). In June 1808, the II Bn escaped but was dispersed. I & III Bns joined the Army of Andalusia. Fought at Bailén (19 July), Tudela (23 Nov). In 1809, the I & II Bns were almost destroyed at Uclés (13 Jan) where The regiment was reduced by half. It later fought at Talavera (27 July) and Ocaña (18-19 Nov). In 1810, it was part of the defence of Cádiz. In 1811, the regiment fought at Barrosa (Chiclana; 5 Mar), Sagunto (25 Oct) and Murviedro (24 Nov). It was part of the defence of Valencia (3 Nov 1811-8 Jan 1812).

Shield - White field with an African on foot armed with a spear or bow in his right hand and severed head in the left hand.

Rgto de América (Est. 1711)

In 1711, the *Rgto Real de América* was formed under D. Miguel Porcel y Manrique and embarked immediately to the city of Veracruz. On 8 August 1764, the regiment was renamed *Rgto de América*. In Dec 1808, I & II Bns were used to form the new *Rgto de la Reunión de Aragón* in Saragossa (*Zaragoza*). On 2 May 1814, the regiment was renamed *Rgto de Infantería América*. Absorbed *Cazadores de Mallorca* (8 Oct 1811) on 2 March 1815.

Campaign History: From 1764 until 1771, the regiment was in Central America, garrison of Mexico City in New Spain (1764-71). Fought at Puebla de Los Angeles (1766), reconquest of Minorca (1781) and siege of Gibraltar (1782). During the war with France (1793-95), they fought at Hendaye, San Juan, Château-Pignon, Monte Mendale and Alcobeta-Alta. In 1797, the regiment defended Santa Cruz de Tenerife against British landings. Defence of Cádiz (1800). War with Portugal (1801). Detachments of the regiment acted as Marines at Trafalgar (21 Oct 1805). In May 1808, the I Bn was in Aranjuez at the confluence of the Tagus and Jarama rivers, 48 km from Toledo and 48 km south of Madrid. The II & III Bns were in the Mediterranean port of Alicante (808 men). In June 1808, joined the Army of Valencia, the I & II Bns fought at Tudela (23 Nov). On 15 Dec 1808, the III Bn in Alicante had 419 men. In 1809, the II-III Bn fought at Alcañiz (23 May), María de Huerva (15-16 June) and Belchite (18 June). In 1813, the regiment was dispatched to capture of the city of Montevideo in Uruguay.

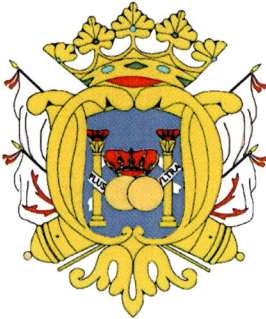

Shield - Sky blue field with waves in the lower part, and two spheres under a Royal crown, between two columns of Hercules surmounted by crown and with the "*PLUS ULTRA*" in black lettering on a white ribbon.

Rgto de America

Rgto de Aragón (Est. 1711)

In 1711, formed in Saragossa under Don Manuel de Sada y Antiñon. The regiment absorbed *Rgto de Molina* (Est. 1705) in 1715 and *Rgto de Barcelona* (Est. 1718) on 23 October 1734. Absorbed *Tiradores de Busa* (1 Nov 1811) and *9º Vol. de Navarra* (Est. 25 Feb 1813) on 2 March 1815.

Rgto de Aragón (Est. 1711)

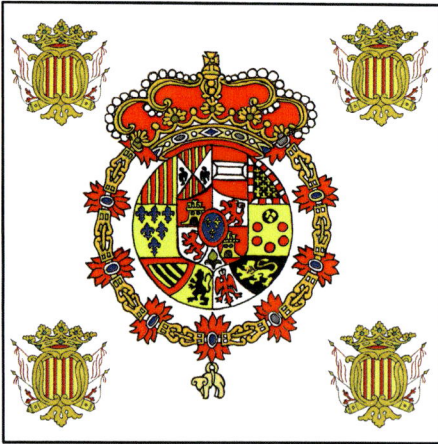

M1762 Coronela Flag

1762 Sencilla Flag

Campaign History: Served in Columbia (1741). War with Portugal (1762) and reconquest of Orán. Garrison of Louisiana (1769-70). Garrison of Cuba (1771-74). Fought at the battle of Algiers and defence of Melilla (1775-76). Siege and capture of Pensacola (9 Mar-8 May 1781). In Santo Domingo for the invasion of Jamaica (1782). Roussillon Campaign (1793-95). In May 1808, the I-II Bns in Viana in Portugal and III Bn in Ferrol, at Puente de Eume (1,296 men). The III Bn joined the Army of Galicia and fought at Medina de Rioseco (14 July), Zornoza (30 Oct) and Espinosa (12 Nov). The remnants fought at La Trepa (6 Mar 1809).

Rgto de Aragón (Est. 1711)

Shield - Yellow with four red bands.

~ 44 ~

Rgto de Asturias (Est. 1703)

The *Tercio de Asturias* was formed in Asturias by *Maestre de Campo* Don Alvaro Navia-Osorio y Vigil on 6 June 1703. In 1707, the regiment was renamed *Rgto de Infantería Asturias*. Absorbed *1º-3º Rgto de Asturias* (Est. 8 May 1812) and *3º Tiradores de Castilla* (Est. 1 Sept 1811) on 2 March 1815.

Campaign History: Garrison of Mexico City in New Spain (1777-84). The regiment participated in the Roussillon Campaign and in many actions in the Western Pyrenees (1793-95). In May 1808, it was in Denmark and was captured by the French (2,103 men). In 1811, the regiment was re-raised. It fought in the defence of Puerto de Pajares in the Province of Asturias, reconquest of Astorga, at battles of Bayonne (9-13 Dec 1813) and Toulouse (10 Apr 1814). Served in Mexico (1816-22).

Shield - Blue field with a cross bracketed by two angles.

**Rgto de Asturias
(Est. 1703)**

Rgto de Borbón (Est. 1796)

In March 1793, the *Legión Real de los Pirineos* was formed from French émigrés and was soon renamed *Légion Católica y Real De Los Pirineos*. In the summer of 1794, these were merged with *Real Rosellón* (Est. June 1793) to become *Legión de la Reina*. On 10 February 1796, *Rgto de Borbón* was formed from French émigré units of *Legión de Saint-Simon*, *Legión de la Reine*, and *Vallespir* by *Maestre de Campo* Don Claudio Rouvroy, Marqués de Saint Simon. Absorbed *1° Rgto de Guipúzcoa* (20 Aug 1810) on 2 March 1815.

**Rgto de Borbón
(Est. 1796)**

Campaign History: All these units were heavily engaged in the Roussillon Campaign (1793-95). In May 1808, the I Bn was in Villa Carlós and the II & III Bns were in Palma in the Balearic Islands (1,544 men). Joined the Army of Catalonia and took part in the defence of Rosas (7 Nov-5 Dec). The regiment fought at the defence of Gerona (6 June-10 Dec 1809). Dissolved by Royal Decree of 1 June 1818.

Shield - Blue field with three *fleurs-a-lis*.

Rgto de Burgos (Est. 1694)

The *Tercio Provincial Nuevo de Burgos* was formed on 2 May 1694. Absorbed *Tiradores de Ledesma* (Est. 1 June 1808) on 15 January 1809. Absorbed *Vol. de Burgos* (Est. 26 Nov 1809) on 25 Oct 1811. Absorbed *Tiradores del Bureva* (Est. 25 Sept 1809) and *3° Tiradores de Cantabria* (Est. 8 May 1812) on 2 March 1815.

Campaign History: War with Portugal (1762-63). Campaign in Algiers (1775). Siege of Gibraltar and re-conquest of Minorca (1780-81). Acted as Marines at

Rgto de Burgos (Est. 1694)

Trafalgar (21 Oct 1805) and Finisterre (1805). May 1808: I Los Santos; II & III Cádiz (1,264) In June 1808, the I Bn was integrated into the French Army by Junot. The II & III Bns joined the Army of Andalusia. Fought at Bailén (19 July) and Tudela (23 Nov). The I & II Bns were almost destroyed at Uclés (13 Jan 1809) and reduced to one Bn. The regiment was in Venezuela, Ecuador and Chile (1816-24).

Shield - Red with the king's bust holding the sceptre in his right hand, a castle on his breast and the other four corners. The motto around the white edge of the shield reads "*CAPUT CASTELL DE CAMERA REGIA.*"

M1762 Coronela

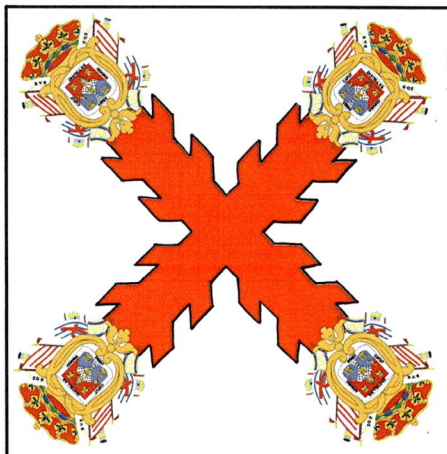

M1762 Sencilla

Rgto de Cantabria (Est. 1703)

The *Tercio de Guipúzcoa* formed in Andalucía under *Maestre de Campo* Don Tomás Idiáquez y Peñarica on 16 May 1703. In 1704 renamed *Rgto de Guipúzcoa*. In 1715, renamed *Rgto de Cantabria*. On 2 March 1812, the regiment absorbed *1° Tiradores de Cantabria* (20 Aug 1809) and *2°-3° Rgto de Iberia* (Est. 15 Sept 1811) then *4° Rgto de Iberia* (Est. 1 May 1812).

Campaign History: Expedition to Algiers (1775). Siege of Gibraltar (1780). Garrison of San Juan in Puerto Rico and Antilles (1790-93). Between 1801 and 1805, acted as Marines at Costa Firme and Cape Finisterre (22 July 1805) off Galicia. In May 1808, the I-III Bns in Ceuta on the northern coast of Africa (1,024 men). The I Bn joined the Army of Andalusia and fought at Bailén (19 July), II & III Bn joined the Army of Castile. The III Bn fought at Tudela (23 Nov) and was defeated at Uclés (13 Jan 1809). In 1809, the remaining battalions fought at Mesa de Ibor (17 Mar), Talavera (27 July), and Ocaña (18-19 Nov). On 5 March 1811, the regiment was present at Barossa (Chiclana) and at the defence of Tarifa (19 Dec 1811-5 Jan 1812). In 1813, it was the garrison of El Puerto de Santa María on the banks of the Guadalete River just 10 km north of Cádiz. In 1814, it was part of the expedition to Chile and Peru until 1824.

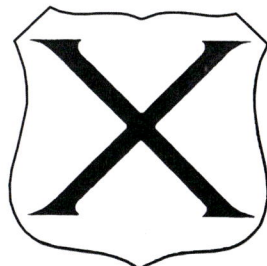

Rgto de Cantabria (Est. 1703)

Shield - White shield with black cross.

Voluntarios de Castilla (Est. 1793)

Formed on 1 June 1793 at the expense of the Duke of Infantado in Leganés and Vicávaro near Madrid. Absorbed *Escolares de Benavente* (Est. 8 June 1808) and *3° Rgto de Guipúzcoa* (20 July 1812) on 2 March 1815.

Voluntarios de Castilla (Est. 1793)

Campaign History: Roussillon Campaign (1794-95). Capitulation of Campo Maior in Portugal (1801). In May 1808, the I-III Bns were in Cartagena (1,487 men). Joined Army of Valencia then fought at Tudela (23-Nov) and in the second siege of Saragossa before surrendering on 21 Feb 1809. In Mexico (1815-21).

Shield - Red shield with yellow castle.

Rgto de Córdoba (Est. 1566)

In 1566, the *Tercio de Figueroa* was formed by Don Lope de Figueroa. In 1603, this became *Tercio Viejo de la Armada Real del Mar Océano* and in 1664, *Tercio Provincial de Córdoba*. On 10 February 1718, *Rgto de Bajeles* became *Rgto de Córdoba*. Absorbed *Vol. de Alicante* (Est. 1 June 1808) on 2 March 1815.

Campaign History: Garrison of Cuba (1763-65). Conquest of the island of Santa Catalina and Sacramento (1777). Siege of Gibraltar and defence of Orán (1779-83).

Rgto de Cordoba (Est. 1566)

In the Roussillon at the siege of Bellegarde (23 May-24 June 1793). In 1805, detachments acted as Marines on Spanish Naval ships at Trafalgar (21 Oct). In May 1808, the I Bn was in Setúbal in Portugal and the II-III Bns in the Isla de León (793 men). Joined Army of Andalusia and fought at Bailén (19 July) and Somosierra (30 Nov). In 1809, fought at Medellín (29 Mar), Almonacid (11 Aug) and Ocaña (18-19 Nov). Then participated in the combats at Castellá (on 21 July 1812 and 13 April 1813).

Shield - Yellow shield with three red horizontal strips.

Rgto de la Corona (Est. 1537)

The *Mar de Nápoles* was formed on 27 February 1537 by Don Pedro Padilla and was transferred to Naples where in 1567, the regiment was renamed *Tercio Nuevo de Nápoles*. In 1704, the regiment became *Regimiento de la Mar de Nápoles*. On 10 February 1718, the regiment became *Rgto de la Corona*.

Campaign History: In Santo Domingo for the abortive invasion of Jamaica (1782). Detachments acted as Marines on Spanish Naval ships at Trafalgar (21 October 1805). In May 1808, the I-III Bns at Algeciras with 902 men joined the Army of Andalusia at Bailén (19 July). The regiment served as the cadre for the new *Rgto de Santa Fe* (Sept 1808). I & III Bns fought at Somosierra (30 Nov) and Uclés (13 Jan 1809). In Peru (1821-1822) then Venezuela and Colombia (1823).

**Rgto de la Corona
(Est. 1537)**

Shield - Blue field with two crossed anchors surmounted by a crown.

Rgto de la Corona (Est. 1537)

M1762 Coronela Flag

M1762 Sencilla Flag

Regimiento de Voluntarios de la Corona (Est. 1795)

LG D. José Urrutia organised *Voluntarios de la Corona* under the command of D. Juan Ordóñez in Madrid on 1 February 1795. On 13 September 1795, it was renamed *Rgto de Cazadores Voluntarios de la Corona*. Absorbed *Vol. de Marchena* (Est. 31 May 1808) on 26 September 1809. In 1815, reorganised as *Rgto de Infantería San Marcial*. Suppressed by Royal Decree of 1 June 1818.

Campaign History: War with Portugal (1801). On 26 August 1802, *Cazadores* was removed from the regiment's title. In 1805, the regiment acted as Marines with

Admiral Gravina at Trafalgar (21 Oct). In May 1808, the I Bn was in Oporto in Portugal and the II-III Bns in Ferrol (1,296 men). Joined the Army of Galicia and fought at capture of Bilbao, Espinosa (14 July), Zornoza (30 Oct) and Medina de Rioseco (10 Nov). In 1813, it exhibited outstanding bravery at battle of San Marcial (31 Aug) after which the regiment was named in 1815. In 1814, fought at Toulouse.

Shield - Royal crown inside of the shield.

Rgto de España (Est. 1660)

Formed in 1660. On 10 February 1718, *Rgto de Córdoba* became *Rgto de España*. Absorbed *Rgto de Almansa* on 15 November 1721. On 28 November 1791, *Rgto de Brabante* was absorbed by *Rgto de España*. Absorbed *6° Vol. de Navarra* (Est. 25 Feb 1813) on 2 March 1815.

Campaign History: From 1741, the regiment served overseas. Louisiana and Western Florida Campaigns (1779-83), Defence of Orán (1790). In 1793-95, the regiment was part of the defence of the central Pyrenees. In May 1808, the I-III Bns were in Ceuta on the northern coast of Africa (1,037 men). Went to the Peninsula and joined the Army of Andalusia. Fought at Medina de Rioseco (14 July 1808), Bailén (19-22 July 1808), Tamames (18 Oct 1809) and Alba de Tormes (26 Nov 1809).

**Rgto de España
(Est. 1660)**

Shield - White field with two spheres under a Royal crown, on blue sea and between two columns crowned with a plinth.

Voluntarios del Estado (Est. 1794)

Formed in 1794 and disbanded in 1808 by the French. After the defeat of the French at Bailén, the Madrid Junta organised *Primer Rgto de Voluntarios de Madrid* on 15 July 1808 from the disbanded regiment commanded by Don António Tomás. In 1810, the regiment was reorganised in Galicia by Colonel Don Manuel Miralles as the *Rgto de Voluntarios de la Victoria*.

Campaign History: In 1803-05, participated in the defence of Ceuta. In 1806, the regiment was in Madrid. In May 1808, the I-III Bns were Madrid (742 men) and were disbanded. *Primer Rgto de Voluntarios de Madrid* fought at Tamames (18 Oct) and was dissolved again after the battle of Tudela (23 Nov). The regiment was later reformed and fought at Vitoria (21 June 1813) Toulouse (10 Apr 1814).

Shield - Royal coat of arms limited to the quartering of Castilla and León, with the grenade on top and the central oval with the *fleurs-de-lis*.

Rgto de Extremadura (Est. 1766)

Rgto Fijo de Badajóz was formed on 15 March 1766 and was renamed *Rgto Fijo de Extremadura* in 1767. In 1769, *Fijo* was removed from the title. Absorbed *Tiradores de Merida* (11 June 1808) on 2 March 1815.

Campaign History: In Santo Domingo for the abortive invasion of Jamaica (1782-90) and Peru (1790). In May 1808, the I-III Bns in Tárraga (770 men). Escaped from Lérida and joined the Army of Aragon. Fought at the first siege of Saragossa (June-Aug) and Tudela (23 Nov). Capitulated at end of the second Siege of Saragossa (21 Nov 1809). Re-raised and was in Mexico (1813-22).

Shield - Red field with the Roman gate of Merida.

Rgto de Extremadura (Est. 1766)

Rgto Fijo de Ceuta (Est. 1703)

The *Tercio Permanente de Ceuta* was formed on 1 August 1703. In 1715, renamed *Rgto de Dotación Fijo de Ceuta*. In 1741, it became the *Rgto de Ceuta Fijo*. In 1769, it was renamed *Rgto Fijo de Ceuta*. On 20 February 1793, the regiment absorbed *Rgto Fijo de Orán* (Est. 9 Jan 1733) as III Bn. The Regulations of 26 August 1802 removed the regiment from the list of line infantry regiments only to be reinstated on 20 December 1804. Absorbed *Rgto Veteranos de la Patria* (Est. 10 Aug 1813) on 2 March 1815. The Royal Decree of 1 June 1818 removed it from the list of line infantry.

Campaign History: Participated in the defence of Ceuta (1751-52). The regiment was part of the reconquest of Minorca, the siege of Gibraltar (1781-82) and the defence of Ceuta (1791). Fought in the Roussillon Campaign (1793-95). In May 1808, I-III Bns were in Ceuta on the northern coast of Africa (1,235 men). I Bn joined the Army of Andalusia and fought at Bailén (19 July) and Lerin (25-26 Oct) and Tudela before returning to Ceuta.

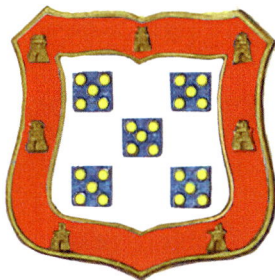

Rgto de Fijo de Ceuta (Est. 1703)

Shield - The coat of arms of Ceuta is a variation of the Portuguese Royal Arms because Ceuta was conquered by Portugal and in 1640 the Portuguese Military Governor decided to side with the Spanish King Philipe IV. White field with five blue escutcheons and in each there were five yellow circles. Around this was a red border with five yellow castles and the motto "*EXPUGNABO INIMICOS FIDEI*" at the bottom.

Rgto de Granada (Est. 1657)

The *Tercio del Casco de Granada* was formed on 22 April 1657. In 1704, renamed *Rgto del Casco de Granada*. Absorbed *Rgto de Granada* (24 June 1808) and *Cazadores Extranjeros* (8 Oct 1812) on 2 March 1815.

Campaign History: Garrison of Vera Cruz in New Spain (1771-84). In the Roussillon Campaign (1793-95), it captured Arlés and Céret, fought at Masdeu, captured Bellegarde and Argelés, fought at Trouillas where it took its name of "*Arrojado*" (the brave one) and at Montesquieu and Pontós. In May 1808, I-III Bns were in Mahon in the Balearic Islands (1,113 men). In July, went on to the Peninsula and joined the Army of Catalonia. Fought at Molins del Rey (21 Dec). In 1809, it fought at Alcañiz (23 May), María de Huerva (15-16 June) and Belchite (18 June). It participated in the Siege of Tarragona (5 May-29 June 1811) where the regiment was destroyed. In 1812, I Bn was re-raised in Palma and II Bn in the island of León. In 1813, it was sent overseas. In 1815, the Regiment was formed in Cádiz with I & III Bns in the Peninsula and II Bn overseas in Venezuela and Colombia.

Rgto de Granada (Est. 1657)

Shield - White field with a pomegranate.

Rgto de Guadalajara (Est. 1657)

The *Tercio de Benevento* was formed on 2 February 1657. In 1710, renamed *Rgto de Guadalajara*. Captured by the French in Denmark in 1808 and the men were formed into the Joseph Napoléon Regiment organised by Don Juan Kindelan. In 1810, the regiment was re-raised in Spain from the *Reunión Murciana*. Absorbed *Rgto de Vélez-Málaga* (Est. 7 June 1808) on 1 March 1810. Absorbed *Rgto de Badajóz* (Est. 2 June 1808) and *Vol. de Molina* (2 June 1810) on 2 March 1815, and *2° Cazadores de Antequera* on 15 November 1815.

Campaign History: Garrison of Louisiana (1769-70) and Cuba (1770-74). Conquest of Santa Catalina, Sacramento, Pensacola and Isla Providencia (1777-80). In Santo Domingo for the invasion of Jamaica (1782). In the Roussillon Campaign (1793-95), the regiment was part of the defence of Figueras and fought at the battles of Bascará and Pontós. In May 1808, it was in Denmark (2,069 men) where it was captured by the French. In 1810, the re-raised regiment participated in the defence of Cádiz (1810-12) and battle of San Marcial. In 1812-13, it was part of Whittingham Brigade, Division of Mallorca.

Rgto de Guadalajara (Est. 1657)

Shield - Ducal crown inside of the shield.

Rgto de Guadalajara (Est. 1657)

Rgto de Jaén (Est. 1793)

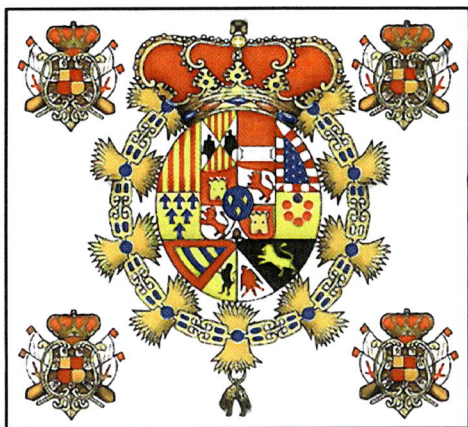

**Coronela of the
Rgto de Jaen (Est. 1793)**

Formed on 1 March 1793 in Seville. In 1810, disbanded. In 1814, re-raised. Absorbed *Rgto de Depósito de San Fernando* (Est. 8 May 1812) on 2 March 1815.

Campaign History: War with France (1794-95), defence of Colliure, defence of Oriol, Villanueva, combat on the heights of Azcárate, Villareal de Zumárraga and Revenga. In May 1808, the I-II Bns were in San Rogue and III Bn in Ceuta on the northern coast of Africa (1,755 men). Joined the Army of Andalusia and fought at Bailén (19 July). The I & III Bns fought at Somosierra (30 Nov). In September 1808, the II Bn was absorbed by the *Rgto Hibernia*. In 1809, fought at Medellín (29 Mar), Talavera (27 July), the blockade of Toledo and battles of Almonacid (11 Aug) and Ocaña (18-19 Nov).

Shield - Quartered shield, the 1st and 4th red, and 2nd and 3rd white, separated by a green cross, and with alternate fringe of yellow castles in red and from León field red in white field.

~ 53 ~

Rgto de León (Est. 1694)

The *Tercio Provincial Nuevo de León* was formed in Corunna, by *Maestre de Campo* D. José Vélez de Cosío on 10 June 1694. In 1697, renamed *Tercio Provincial de los Colorados*. In 1700, the regiment became *Tercio de los Amarillos Nuevos*. In 1704, renamed *Rgto Provincial de León*. In 1707, the regiment became *Rgto de León*. In 1809, the remnants were renamed *Bn de Tiradores del Bierzo*. In 1812, the regiment was re-raised as *Rgto de León*. Absorbed *3º Rgto de Viscaya* (Est. 1 Mar 1812) on 2 March 1815.

**Rgto de Leon
(Est. 1694)**

Campaign History: Garrison of San Juan in Puerto Rico (1766-68). In Santo Domingo for the abortive invasion of Jamaica (1782-83). Roussillon Campaign (1793-95) in the defence of San Sebastián. Defence of the city of Ferrol (1800). In May 1808, the I Bn was in Corunna; II Bn in Vivarium and III Bn in Northern Portugal (1,195). In June, the I Bn went to Oporto to support the Portuguese uprising lead by the Bishop of Oporto and received in Noevember the *Ordem Militar da Torre e Espada do Valor, Lealdade e Mérito*[98] (the "Portuguese Star") that they embroidered on their left arm. The II & III Bns joined the Army of Galicia and fought at Medina de Rioseco (14 July), and III Bn at Espinosa (12 Nov) and Mansilla (29 Dec) where the regiment was mauled. In 1809, it fought at Tamames (18 Oct). The re-raised regiment fought at Nive (9-13 Dec 1813) and Toulouse (10 Apr 1814).

Shield White with red lion rampant.

Rgto de Málaga (Est. 1790)

Rgto Fijo de Málaga of 2 Bns was formed by Royal Order on 15 July 1790 but did not begin to form until 24 September. In 1793, renamed *Rgto de Málaga*.

Campaign History: War with France (1793-95) in the expedition to Toulon. Defence of Melilla (1796-1806). In May 1808, the I-III Bns were in Málaga (854 men). Joined the Army of Andalusia and fought at the Almonacid (11 Aug 1809) and in the defence of Cádiz (5 Feb 1810-25 Aug 1812).

Shield - Walled city by the sea with the wall stretching to the top of the hill on which there is a virgin between two saints.

**Rgto de Malaga
(Est. 1790)**

---

[98] The translation is "Military Order of the Tower and of the Sword, of Valour, Loyalty and Merit." This is the highest Portuguese honour created by King Afonso V in 1459. It was revived in November 1808 to commemorate the safe arrival of the Royal Family in Brazil for both Portuguese and foreigners for military, political or civilian achievement irrespective of religion.

Rgto de Mallorca (Est. 1682)

The *Tercio Nuevo de la Armada y del Mar Océano* was formed on 18 June 1682. On 10 February 1718, *Rgto de Armada* became *Rgto de Mallorca*. Absorbed *2° Rgto de Vizcaya* (Est. 1 Mar 1812) on 2 March 1815.

Campaign History: In America (1765-81) captured Sacramento, invaded Florida, Captured Fort Bute (7 Sept 1779), Captured Baton Rouge and Fort Panmure at Natchez (13 Sept 1779), siege and capture of Fort Charlotte, Mobile (1-14 Mar 1780), siege and capture of Pensacola (9 Mar-8 May 1781). In Africa 1785-90, fought in Algiers, in the defence of Orán and Nacimiento. War with France (1793-95), captured Ceret, battles of Masdeu and Thuir, defence of Toulon, Trompete, Montesquieu, the St Lawrence of the Muga, defence of Báscara and battle of Pontós. The regiment participated in the war with Portugal (1801). In May 1808, the I-II Bns were in Oporto in Portugal and III Bn in Badajóz (1,749 men). In June, the III Bn became *2° Rgto de Mallorca*. I-II Bns joined the Army of Galicia, resulting in great loss at Medina de Rioseco (14 July) and Zornoza (30 Oct). Reorganised into 3 Bns, 2 Bns fought at Gamonal (10 Nov). I Bn fought in Espinosa (12 Nov). In 1809, the remnants fought at La Trepa (6 Mar). II Bn fought at Medellín (29 Mar) and Talavera (27 July).

Shield - Yellow with four red bars and a diagonal blue band.

Rgto de Mallorca
(Est. 1682)

Rgto de Murcia (Est. 1694)

Rgto de Murcia
(Est. 1694)

The *Tercio Provincial Nuevo de Murcia* was formed on 25 May 1694. Absorbed *Cazadores de Bailén* (Est. 14 Sept 1808) on 15 January 1809. Absorbed *Cazadores de Llerena* (Est. 31 May 1808) and *Cazadores de las Navas de Tolosa* (Est. 14 Sept 1809) on 1 March 1809. Absorbed *Vol. de Jaén* (11 July 1811), *5° Vol. de Navarra* (Est. 28 Sept 1811) and *2° Rgto de Cádiz* (8 May 1812) on 2 March 1815.

Campaign History: The regiment participated in the defence of the Havana, Cuba (1760-62), the war with Portugal (1762-69), expedition to Algiers (1775), actions in the area of Montevideo and Rio de la Plata (1777), expedition to Ireland (1779), siege of Gibraltar and reconquest of Minorca (1781-82) and the defence of Orán (1791-92). In 1793-95 against France, it fought at Castel-Pignon and Valcarlos. In May 1808, the I-II

Bns were in Setúbal in Portugal with the French and III Bn in San Roque (1,762 men). The I-II Bns managed to escape despite their Colonel Galbán siding with the French and joined the III Bn in the Army of Andalusia. Fought at Bailén (19 July), Tudela (23 Nov). Almost destroyed at Uclés (13 Jan 1809) and later fought at Mesa de Ibor (17 Mar 1809), Barrosa (Chiclana: 5 Mar 1811) and Albuera (16 May 1811).

Shield - Red with six golden crowns, and in the centre a heart crowned formed by a white edge with the motto *"PRISCAE NOVISSLMA EXALTAT ET AMOR"* with a gold lion and *fleur-a-lis* in his interior. Around border it alternates of Castile and León.

Rgto de Navarra

Rgto de Navarra (Est. 1705)

The *Tercio del Condestable de Navarra* (Est. 1632) became on 20 September 1705, the *Rgto de Navarra*. It absorbed *Rgto de Valladolid* on 23 October 1734. Absorbed *1º Rgto de Vizcaya* (Est. 1 July 1810) and *Tiradores de Cuenta* (15 Aug 1811) on 2 March 1815.

Campaign History: Garrison of Cuba (1779-83). The regiment participated in the siege and capture of Fort Charlotte, Mobile (1-14 Mar 1780), the siege and capture of Pensacola (9 Mar-8 May 1781). On May 1808, the I-III Bns were in La Coruña (822 men). Joined the Army of Galicia and fought at Medina de Rioseco (14 July), Valmaceda (5 Nov), Espinosa (10-11 Nov) and almost destroyed at Mansilla de las Mulas (30 Dec).

Shield - Red with the chains of Navarre and a green emerald in the centre.

Rgto de Navarra (Est. 1705)

Rgto de Órdenes Militares (Est. 1793)

Formed by Don António Fernández of Córdoba y Pimentel, Duke of Arión on 20 June 1793, the I Bn in Leganés and the II & III Bns in Ocaña.

Campaign History: War with France (1793-95), I Bn at the battle of Colliure. In 1799-1803, fought at Doniños, defence of El Ferrol and Cádiz. In May 1808, the I Bn was in Badajóz and II-III Bns in Cádiz (708). Joined the Army of Andalusia and fought at Bailén (19 July), Lerin (25-26 Oct), Tudela (23 Nov), and Bubierca (29 Nov). The I-III Bns were almost destroyed at Uclés (13 Jan 1809). In Mexico (1815-1822).

**Coronela of the
Rgto de Ordenes Militares
(Est. 1793)**

Shield - White quartered shield the 1st quarter red Santiago Cross, the 2nd green Alcántara Cross, the 3rd red Calatrava Cross and the 4th Montesa Cross.

Rgto de la Princesa (Est. 1765)

Formed under D. Carlos Manuel Dongo on 19 December 1765. Absorbed *1° Tiradores de Castilla* (Est. 3 June 1808) and *1° Rgto de Rivero* (Est. 19 Aug 1808) on 2 March 1815.

Campaign History: War in Africa (1774). War in America (1777-78). Reconquest of Minorca (1781-82). Siege of Gibraltar (1782). Roussillon Campaign (1793-95). In May 1808, the regiment was in Denmark (1,969 men). In October 1808, joined the Army of Galicia and fought at Valmaceda (5 Nov), Espinosa (10-11 Nov). In 1809, part of La Romana's successful raid on *6e Ligne* who garrisoned Villafranca (17 Mar), Gallegos (19 May), and at Alba de Tormes. In 1810-11, two Bns were part of the defence of Lines of Torres Vedras. In 1811, one Bn was in 2nd (Virues) Division of Mendizabal's Army of Extremadura that was defeated at Río Gévora (19 Feb).

Two Bns were present at Sagunto. In 1812, part of de España Division of the 4th Army.

Shield - Red with the golden Cross of Victoria.

Rgto del Príncipe (Est. 1537)

On 6 November 1537, *Tercio Ordinario del Estado de Milán* was formed by Don Rodrigo de Ripalda. The regiment became *Rgto del Príncipe* in 1765. In 1808, amalgamated with *Rgto Alcázar de San Juan* and *Tercero de Voluntarios de Navarra*. In 1818, amalgamated with *Rgto de Borbón*.

Campaign History: Conquest of Mobile (1768-70) and garrison of Cuba (1771-79). In November 1776, the regiment disappeared from the Infantry lists and became a Battalion of Marines. Fought in the Louisiana and Western Florida Campaigns (1779-83) at the capture of Fort Bute (7 Sept 1779), Baton Rouge and Fort Panmure at Natchez (13 Sept 1779), the siege and capture of Fort Charlotte, Mobile (1-14 March 1780), siege and capture of Pensacola (9 Mar-8 May 1781). Roussillon Campaign (1793-95). In May 1808, the I-II Bns were in Valença do Minho in Portugal and III Bn in La Coruña (1,267 men). The I-III Bns joined the Army of Galicia and fought at Tamames and 2 Bns at Medina de Rioseco (14 July 1808) and Zornoza (30 Oct). The regiment fought at Mesa de Ibor (17 Mar 1809) then in the defence of Ciudad Rodrigo (1810) and Badajóz (1811).

Rgto de Princesa
in M1805 uniform

Shield - Monogram between two lions, surrounded a necklace and under royal crown.

Rgto de la Reina [also de la Reyna] (Est. 1509)

In 1509, the *Tercio de Lombardía* was formed. In 1705, this became the *Rgto de Lombardía*. In 1712, became *Rgto de Galicia*. In 2 September 1792, the *Rgto de Galicia* was renamed *Rgto de la Reina*.[99] In 1810, the I and II Bns were formed from *Milicia Provincial* (Provincial Militia). On 3 March 1811, the regiment was renamed to *Rgto de Galicia*. Absorbed *1º Cazadores de Valencia* (Est. 17 May 1808) and *2º Vol. de Sevilla* (Est. 30 May 1808) on 2 March 1815.

Campaign History: Capture of Almeida and Alcântara (1762-63). Capture of the Island of Santa Catalina and Sacramento (1776-77). In the Roussillon Campaign (1793-95), it fought at Villafranca, Bellegarde, the capture of Santelmo and Colibre, the battles of Boló and Figueras (Figueres in Catalonian). In May 1808, the I-III Bns were in Málaga (1530 men). Joined the Army of Andalucía and fought at Bailén

---

[99] The original *Rgto de la Reina* was created in Guadalajara on 1 April 1735 and was dissolved on 24 October 1769 for inciting to mutiny.

(19 July). Later the Bns were separated. I Bn fought in Tudela (23 Nov). The II & III Bn fought at Somosierra (30 Nov 1808). The I Bn annihilated at Uclés (13 Jan 1809). The regiment fought at Almonacid (11 Aug 1809). Fought at Vitoria (21 June 1813).

Shield - The ciphers of the Queen of Spain. Note *Rgto de Galicia* had a white field with chalice.

Rgto del Rey (Ancient)

The regiment is considered to be the oldest regiment in the world. In 1248 Ferdinand III of Castile conquered Seville and instead of disbanding *Banda de Castilla* as was the practice at the time, the King decided to permanently retain the regiment. On 28 August 1632, Philip IV ordered the formation of a unit of veteran soldiers (*Unidad de la Ciudad de Almansa*). In 10 September 1634, fifteen companies of 90 harquebusiers, 40 musketeers, and 60 pikemen were formed at Almansa under Don Gaspar de Guzmán, Duke of Olivares. In 1638, the regiment was augmented to twenty companies. In 1640, Philip IV elevated it to a *Regimiento de la Guardia del Rey* which had the privilege to guard the king until 1662 and in 1664 the regiment was renamed *Tercio de Castilla*. In 1668, the regiment was named *Tercio de Infantería Española Provincial de Sevilla* and popularly *Tercio de los Morados* due to the colour of their uniform. From 1701-10, it guarded the Monarch and in 1710 the regiment was renamed *Rgto de Castilla Inmemorial*. It was distinguished in the War of Spanish Succession and the Italian Campaigns (1718-1749). On 23 October 1734, the regiment absorbed *Rgto de Badajóz*. On 6 January 1766, the regiment was named *Rgto Inmemorial del Rey* as Charles III acknowledged their antiquity. The II Bn was named *Bn Infantería of Príncipe* by Order of 2 December 1812. Absorbed *1° Rgto de Guadix* (Est. 10 Aug 1808) on 2 March 1815.

M1762 Coronela   M1762 Sencilla

Regimento del Rey

Campaign History: The regiment participated in the siege and capitulation of Almeida (1762). The regiment was part of the defence of Algiers (1775), conquest of Pensacola, fortresses of Media Luna and San Jorge, assisted Puerto Rico and conquest of San Agustín (1781-82) and Roussillon Campaign (1793-94). In May 1808, the I Bn was in San Sebastián and was captured by the French, the II Bn was in Oporto and the III Bn in Ares (1,353 men). The II &III Bns joined the Army of Galicia where they fought at Medina de Rioseco (14 July) and Zornoza (30 Oct). The regiment was joined by a newly raised I Bn at Espinosa (10 Nov) and Foncedadon where the regiment was taken prisoner. The regiment fought at Tamames (18 Oct 1809 and at Albuera (16 May 1811).

Shield - Red with yellow castle.

Rgto de Saboya (Est. 1537)

In 1537, *Tercio de Saboya* was formed by Don Rodrigo López de Ouirogo. On 30 March 1633, the regiment became *Tercio de Lombardía* in Cremona in Italy. In 1702, the regiment was amalgamated with *Rgto de la Victoria*. In 1706, the regiment was transferred to Spain. In 1718, renamed *Rgto de Saboya*.

Grenadier
flame of
Rgto de Saboya
By Vaughan Funnell

Rgto de Saboya
(Est. 1537)

Standard bearer with Sencilla
of Rgto de Saboya, 1808

Campaign History: Garrison of Mexico City in New Spain (1768-73) and Venezuela (1774-80). Captured la Paz, Mexico (1780). In May 1808, the I Bn was in Vallecas and II-III Bns in Valencia (936 men). Joined the Army of Valencia, but soon afterwards II Bn joined the Army of Catalonia. The I Bn fought at Tudela (23 Nov). The III Bn fought at Alcañiz (23 May 1809) and Belchite (18 June 1809). The II Bn capitulated at Saragossa (21 Nov 1809). In Mexico (1813-21).

Shield - Red with white cross.

Rgto de Sevilla (Est. 1657)

The *Tercio de Infantería de la Armada del Mar Océano* was formed on 20 February 1657. In 1664, renamed *Tercio Provincial de Madrid*. In 1802, reorganised in Ferrol into 3 Bns after overseas service. Absorbed *2° Rgto de Guipúzcoa* (1 Sept 1810) on 2 March 1815.

Campaign History: War with Portugal (1762). Garrison of Cuba (1770). Defence of Algiers (1775). Conquest of the island of Santa Catalina, Sacramento, islands of Fernando Pó and Martín García (1777-78). Participated in the battles of St Louis (26 May 1780), St Joseph (2 Jan 1781), captured Fort Natchez (Mar 1781) and Pensacola (9 Mar-8 May 1781). Siege of Gibraltar (1782-83). Defence of Ceuta (1790). Roussillon Campaign (1793-95). In May 1808, the I-III Bns were in Ferrol (1,168 men). Joined the Army of Galicia and fought at Medina de Rioseco (14 July) where the regiment lost a sixth of its strength, Espinosa (10-11 Nov) and then at Zorzona (31 Oct). The IV Bn was almost destroyed at Uclés (13 Jan 1809) and fought at Medellín (29 Mar 1809).

Shield - White shield with King San Fernando with a sword in his right hand.

Rgto de Soria (Est. 1591)

In 1591, the *Tercio Departamental de Bramante* was formed. In 1715, it was renamed *Rgto de Infantería Soria*. Absorbed *Rgto de Ausona* (Est. 8 Aug 1811) on 23 November 1813.

Campaign History: Blockade of Gibraltar (1779-81), expedition to Pensacola (9 Mar-8 May 1781), in Santo Domingo for the abortive invasion of Jamaica (1782) and put down the riot of Tupac Amarú in Peru (1783-87). War of the Pyrenees (1793-94) where the regiment occupied Bellegarde and defended Figueras (Figueres in Catalonian). In 1805, detachments acted as Marines at Trafalgar (21 Oct). In May 1808, the I-III Bns were in Mahon, Balearic Islands (1,311 men). Went to the Peninsula and joined the Army of Catalonia. Fought at

Rgto de Soria
(Est. 1591)

Cardedeu (16 Dec 1808), Valls (25 Feb 1809) and at the defence of Tortosa (16 Dec 1810-2 Jan 1811) the regiment was captured. Those that escaped were reorganised into the *Rgto de Ausona* that fought at Altafulla (24 Jan 1812).

Shield - Red with a King on the battlements of a yellow castle surrounded by a white fringe with the motto *"SORLA PURA CABEZA DE EXTREMADURA."*

Rgto de Toledo (Est. 1661)

Rgto de Toledo
in M1805 uniform

The *Tercio de Vera* was formed by D. Diego Fernández de Vera on 1 May 1661. In 1693, renamed *Tercio Provincial de los Azules Viejos*. In 1707, it became the *Rgto de Infantería Toledo*. In 1715, it was amalgamated with *Rgto Sada y Limburgo*. Reformed on 2 March 1815 from *Vol. de Rioja* (6 Sept 1810).

Campaign History: Fought in Orán, Africa (1756). In the Caribbean at the battle of Puerto Rico and the defence of Havana in Cuba (1760-64), garrison of San Juan in Puerto Rico (1769-70), defence of Algiers (1775), expedition of Ceballos to Mar de la Plata (1777), conquest of island of Santa Catalina (1778), Sacramento (1780) and Florida de Santa Pola (1777-1780), siege and capture of Pensacola (9 Mar-8 May 1781). 1781-82, reconquest of the island of Minorca (1781-82). II Bn acted as Marines and posted to Santo Domingo (1781-82). Roussillon Campaign (1793-95) at the action of Castel Pignon. In May 1808, the I Bn was in La Coruña, II Bn in Vivero and III Bn in Caminas in Portugal (1,058 men). Joined the Army of Galicia and lost 400 men at Medina de Rioseco (14 July 1808). Then fought at Zornoza (30 Oct) and Espinosa (12 Nov), Tamames (18 Oct 1809), defences of Cáceres (1810) and Badajóz (1811) where it was completely destroyed.

Shield - The first and fourth quarter was red with a yellow castle. The second and third was white with lion rampant red.

Rgto de Valencia (Est. 1658)

On 22 September 1658, the *Milicias de la Costa de Granada* (Est. 1557), and the *Tercio Ordinario de las Milicias de la Costa de Granada* (Est. 1558) were combined. In 1718, it was renamed *Rgto de Vitoria*. In 1791, renamed *Rgto de Valencia*.[100] On 2 March 1815, it was reformed from the *2° Rgto del Príncipe* (Est. 15 July 1808), *Rgto de Almería* (Est. 1 Sept 1808) and *Rgto de Depósito de San Fernando* (Est. 8 May 1812).

Campaign History: The regiment took part in the Roussillon Campaign against France (1793-95). In May 1808, I-III Bns were in the important naval port

Rgto de Valencia
(Est. 1658)

---

[100] The original *Rgto de Valencia* was created on 1 May 1735 and was suppressed at the end of 1739 or beginning of 1740.

of Cartagena in the Province of Murcia on the Mediterranean coast, south-eastern Spain (923 men). Upon joining the Army of Valencia in June, the regiment was renamed *1° de Valencia* and fought at Tudela (23 Nov) before withdrawing into Valencia. From 3 November 1811, the regiment participated in the defence of Valencia until 8 January 1812 when it was dissolved upon the capture of the city.

Shield - Inherited the *Rgto de Victoria* emblem of a crown of green laurels tied with red ribbon.

M1762 Coronela

M1762 Sencilla

Regimiento de Valencia

Rgto de Zamora (Est. 1580)

In 1704, *Rgto de Zamora* was raised. In 1713, the *Tercio de Bobadilla* (Est. 30 April 1580 from natives of the province of Zamora) and *Tercio de las Azores* (Est. c1582) were combined to form the *Rgto de Zamora*. In 1718, the regiment absorbed the *Rgtos de Mondoñedo* and *de Compostela*. The II Bn of this Regiment was named *Bn Infantería de Saboya* by Order of 24 December 1812. Absorbed *Cazadores de Carmona* (Est. 11 June 1808), and *Rgto del Fen. De la Reserva de Andalucía* (Est. 24 Feb 1813) on 2 March 1815.

Campaign History: The regiment participated in the victories in Salvaterra and at Almeida (1762), the conquest of Sacramento (1777), in Santo Domingo for the invasion of Jamaica (1782) and as garrison of Vera Cruz in New Spain (1783-89). In May 1808, in Denmark (2,096 men) and 12 September returned to Spain to join 5th (La Romana) Division of Army of Galicia. The regiment fought at Valmaceda (5 Nov), and 3 Bns at Espinosa (10-11 Nov). In 1809, the

Rgto de Zamora
[Richard Knotel]

remnants fought at La Trepa (6 Mar). The regiment was part of La Romana's successful raid on *6e Ligne* who garrisoned Villafranca (17 Mar). Fought at Gallegos (19 May), Alba de Tormes (I-II Bn). In 1810-11, the regiment was part of defence of the Lines of Torres Vedras. One Bn was in 2nd (Virues) Division of Mendizabal's Army of Extremadura that was defeated at Río Gévora (19 Feb 1811) and another Bn at Albuera (16 May 1811).

Shield - A plate armoured hand holding a flag with red, white and blue horizontal stripes.

Grenadier flame of Rgto de Zamora
By Vaughan Funnell

Rgto de Zaragoza (Est. 1660)

Form in 1579 as the *Tercio de los Niño*. In 1713, the regiment was renamed *Rgto de Infantería Lisboa*. On 21 June 1791, the *Rgto de Lisboa* was renamed *Rgto de Zaragoza*.

Campaign History

From 1741-70, the regiment was in the Americas as garrison of Cuba (1765-69) and Louisiana (1769-70). In 1790, the regiment participated in the defence of Orán. In 1793-95, the regiment defended the central Pyrenees. In May 1808, the I-II Bns were in Oporto in Portugal and the III Bn in Cádiz (1,561 men). The I-II Bns joined the Army of Galicia and fought at Medina de Rioseco (14 July), Zorzona (31 Oct) and Espinosa (10 Nov). The III Bn joined the Army of Andalusia and fought at Bailén (19 July), Zornoza (30 Oct) and Tudela (23 Nov). In 1809, the regiment fought at Tamames (18 Oct) and Alba de Tormes (26 Nov). Later dissolved to create the *Rgto. Almería*.

Shield - Red field with yellow lion rampant.

Spanish Firearms

In 1719, the *Real Fábrica de Armas en Silillos* in Madrid was founded. In 1753, the *Real Compañía de Caracas* was put in charge of the manufacture of arms for the Spanish Army and greatly improved the quality of weapons.[101]

In 1774, the Royal Factory of Placencia[102] was established. The dominance of the Catalonian firearms makers was broken by the decision of the Royal Treasury to suspend the purchase of official firearms 1773-82. The firearms manufacturers in Catalonia survived by supplying individuals with weapons and making *escopetas* muskets for the *Cazadores* light infantry.[103]

From 1784, the *Real Compañía Guipuzcoana de Caracas* was a supplier to the Royal Factory of Placencia. In 1785, the *Real Compañía de Filipas* replaced the *Real Compañía de Caracas* as arms manufacturer.[104]

In 1794, the Royal Factory of Placencia was evacuated and occupied by the French. Many armourers left the area and it was decided in 1795 to establish their first crown owned firearms factory in Asturias called the *Real Fábrica de Oviedo*.[105] Also, the Treasury resumed contracts with the factories in Catalonia but they were unable to supply the numbers of firearms required due to the severe reduction in the number of armourers. They were reduced to repairing and re-stocking firearms.[106]

After the start of the Peninsular War, the French quickly occupied the armament and munitions factories of Placencia, Catalonia, Oviedo and Toledo. As a result the armourers who evacuated or fled were employed to set up new factories in territories not controlled by the invader in Seville, Cádiz, Granada, Jerez de la Frontera, Murcia, Valencia and Berga. Ultimately only those in Cádiz and Ceuta escaped French occupation.

The most important Spanish production centres were Seville (to 31 Jan 1810),[107] Valencia (to 9 Jan 1812)[108] and Cádiz (never occupied). As a result of difficulties in procuring sufficient funds and resources for manufacture, the Spanish relied increasingly upon weapons supplied by the British such as the East India Pattern and old Tower Pattern "Brown Bess" muskets, carbines and pistols, and M1792 light cavalry sabres. The better quality muskets were reserved for the better units.[109]

---

[101] Hernadez Pardo (1984) V: p58
[102] Referred to as the *"RR.FF. de Placencia"* in Spanish.
[103] Calvó Pascal (2008) p13
[104] Hernadez Pardo (1984) V: p58
[105] Hernadez Pardo (1984) V: p59
[106] Calvó Pascal (2008) pp13-14
[107] Lipscombe (2010) p152
[108] Lipscombe (2010) p242
[109] Calvó Pascal (2008) p14

In 1685, the **Spanish Lock (*llava española*)** for the flintlock was introduced. This is commonly referred to by English speaking collectors as the *miquelete*[110] and by the Spanish as the *llava vizcaína*. The most characteristic features associated with the Spanish Lock were the large external mounted main spring and the large ring of the top jaw screw.[111] The Spanish Lock was used up until 1718 when it was replaced by the French Lock. Only Catalan produced weapons persisted with this lock. In 1789 the Spanish Lock was reintroduced as it was considered much stronger than the French style locks.

Spanish Lock from a M1789 Carbine

Table 1: Spanish *Fusils* (Infantry Muskets)[112]

	Calibre	Total length	Barrel length	Lock type	Fittings
M1700 *Fusil*	18.5mm	154cm	113cm	Spanish	Steel
M1718 *Fusil*	18.5mm	154cm	113cm	French	Steel
M1752 *Fusil*	18.5mm	152cm	109cm	French	Steel
M1757 *Fusil*	18mm	148.5cm	109cm	French	Brass
M1772 *Escopeta* Musket	18mm	140cm	99.7cm	Spanish	Brass
M1789 *Fusil*	18mm	150cm	111cm	Spanish	Brass
M1801 *Fusil*	18mm	150cm	111cm	Hybrid	Brass

The Spanish referred to muskets as *Fusils* due to French Bourbon influence on the Spanish court from 1700. The **M1718 *Fusil*** was based on the French M1717 musket. Before 1757, the musket calibre was 18.5mm (0.73in) and other weapons were 16.9mm (0.665in). From 1757, all weapons were 18mm (0.69in).[113]

The new **M1752 *Fusil*** combined the best features of the earlier French and Spanish muskets. It had iron fittings and a wooden rammer. The barrel was octagon to round. The lock plate measured 16.5 x 3cm and the throw of the cock was 5cm. It weighed about 4.1kg. In 1755, the steel ramrod was adopted.

---

[110] *Migueletes* referred to Spanish irregular mountain light infantry supposedly hence their firearm was referred to by the British as the *Miquelet*. The term *miquelet* was not used until after 1815.
[111] Benninghoff (1991) p2
[112] Calvó Pascal (2008) 29-32, 51-52; Benninghoff (1991) 1-6
[113] Calvó Pascal (2008) p15

The **M1757** *Fusil* had brass rather than iron fittings. Interestingly, Carlos III approved four million *reales* in bullion in 1777 for the Americans to purchase arms and uniforms including 30,000 M1757 Spanish muskets with bayonets. This was two years before Spain formerly declared war on Britain.[114]

Spanish M1757 Fusil
Reproduction

The **M1772** *Escopeta* was the standard weapon much favoured by the *Cazadores* (Light Infantry) especially from Catalonia due to it being light and well balanced. The barrel was octagon to a flared round. The stock was considerably slimmer than the other Spanish muskets and hence weighed about 3.2kg. The lock plate measured 14 x 3.5cm. The throw of the cock was 5cm.

Catalonian Escopeta Carbine

In 1789, the Spanish readopted the *miquelete* lock because of its strength and reliability for the **M1789** *Fusil.* The stock was similar to the M1752 with the exception of the lock panel carving being removed. It had an octagon to round barrel. The lock plate measured 14.6 x 3.7cm. The throw of the cock was 6.4cm.

The **M1801** *Fusil* had a new lock.[115] It had the catch of the *miquelete* lock and the internal mainspring from the M1757 Spanish *Fusil.* The fittings were redesigned and simplified. The beach or maple stock was similar to the earlier models but slightly slimmer than the previous models. The barrel was octagon to round. The lock plate measured 16.5 x 3.3cm. The throw of the cock was 3.8cm.

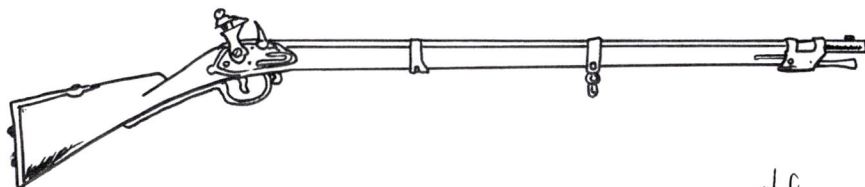

Spanish M1801 Musket

---

[114] Benninghoff (1991) pp1-3
[115] Some authors state this was 1803.

M1797 Fusilier Uniform

Traditionally the Spanish Infantry wore white coats with facing colours on their collars, Swedish cuffs and lapels according to the regiments. Three regiments were still wearing their M1797 uniform in May 1808.

Spanish Cazador and proposed Fusiliers uniform, c1791

The Prussian style mitres were never produced and the uniform was not implemented. By Clonard, 1851

Cazador, Grenadier and Fusilier in M1797 uniform

By Clonard, 1851

M1802 Fusilier Uniform

The Royal Order of 8 June 1802 introduced for the first time a single uniform for all Spanish line infantry. The deep sky blue was a particular favourite of Godoy. A regiment was distinguished by its numbers on the buttons, the grenadier bags and the corner emblems of their flags. The exact shade is the subject to a great deal of controversy. Various sources show the shade from light blue to royal blue. Most of the regiments received their M1802 uniform in 1803-04 except the *Rgtos Ceuta, Málaga* and *Jaén* who were stationed in North Africa. In May 1808, a dozen infantry regiments were still wearing the M1802 uniform.[116]

M1802

Grenadier, Fusilier and Sapper
By Jose Bueno

Summerfield, 2013

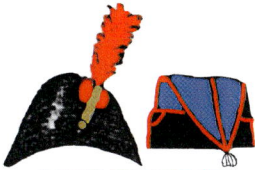

Fusilier

Grenadier

M1802 Infantry Uniform

HEADWEAR: Black felt bicorn with a red cockade, red plume and a loop in regimental colour.

TUNIC: Deep sky blue long tailed coat had black collar, lapels and cuffs with red piping and a *fleur-de-lis* on the collar. Red turnbacks.

LEGWEAR: White breeches, black gaiters and black shoes.

---

[116] *Rgtos del Rey, Reina, Corona, Granada, Zaragoza, España, León, Aragón, Extremadura*, and *los Voluntarios de Castilla, del Estado* and *de la Corona*.

M1802 Bicornes [Suhr]

M1802 Fusilier Jacket

M1802 officer's bicorn

Plate 2: Soldiers of the *Rgto de Guadalajara* and *Militia.*
By Christoph Suhr

A group of four fusiliers all from the *Regimiento de Guadalajara* attired differently in a mixture of full dress, old uniforms and stable dress. Regardless of uniform all men would have jackets with brass buttons stamped with the regimental name to aid in identification (order dated 8 July 1802).

The soldier on the right has the old M1802 uniform distinctive in its shade of deep sky blue, a colour favoured by the Spanish and later by the Mexicans of Santa Anna. Otherwise his scarlet facings match his colleague's red plumes as commonly worn by most fusiliers.

The Provincial Militiaman (left) in brown cloak and brown jacket with scarlet facings edged white, white buttons and the militiaman (right) were attached to the artillery.

The Grenadier (centre left) is in the M1805 barrack dress of white sleeved waistcoat with scarlet facings, white breeches and gaiters. The soldier (centre right) is in the M1805 white uniform with scarlet facings and dark brown gaiters. The black bicorn has a red feather in the red cockade.

Plate 3: Fusiliers of the *Regimientos de Asturias, la Princesa* and *Guadalajara*

By Christoph Suhr

This plate is again a kaleidoscope of coat and colour variations with three infantry regiments in total depicted; *Asturias* (1), *La Princesa* (2, 4, & 6), *Guadalajara* (3) plus the Provincial Militiaman attached to the artillery (5). Blue was a popular colour for Spanish infantry musicians and band members, the cavalry favouring the more exotic red or scarlet.

(1) Fusilier of Rgto de Asturias *in M1805 Uniform:* White jacket with green facings and white buttons. Red cummerbund sash.

(2) Fusilier of the Rgto de la Princesa *smoking a cigarette in M1805 Uniform:* White *bonnet de police* has a light blue rather than violet hat band and the top is piped red. The white waistcoat has a violet collar, white lapels, red sleeve lacing and black pocket patch edged red. He wears white breeches with light green decoration and white stockings. His light brown leather sandals have light green laces.

(3) Rear view of fusilier of Rgto de Guadalajara *M1805 Uniform:* The white *bonnet de police* has scarlet hat band and piping. The white M1805 jacket has scarlet collar, cuffs, lapels, turnbacks and lacing to pockets; and white buttons.

(4) Fusilier Rgto de la Princesa *in M1802 Uniform:* Deep sky blue coat with black facings edged red, yellow buttons and collar badge. Red plume and sash.

(5) Provincial Militiaman attached to the artillery
Deep sky blue coat with scarlet facings and yellow buttons. Red sash. White waistcoat with red piping. Black neck stock. White breeches and gaiters. Black felt bicorn with red plume.

(6) Drummers of Regimiento de la Princesa *in M1802 Uniform*
Deep sky blue coat with scarlet facings and brass buttons. Black neck stock. White breeches and gaiters. Black felt bicorn. The brass drum had black hoops. From the reign of Carlos III, all drummers had blue coats with red facings and turnbacks.[117]

Spanish Infantry Drummer, c1807
[Scharf after Suhr]

---

[117] Luis Sorando Muzas (1/12/2013) *Private Communication.*

Plate 4: Drum-majors and bandsmen of the *Regimientos de la Princesa* and *Zamora*

By Christoph Suhr

Drum-major of *Regimiento de la Princesa* in M1802 Uniform (right): Light blue coat with black facings piped red, white buttons, and yellow collar badge. Red and gold sash. Brown staff with silver knob. Bicorn with red plume. Bandsmen of *Regimiento de Zamora* in M1805 Uniform (centre): The three central musicians have red coats with black facings, swallow's nest, white buttons and white lace. The bicorn had white plumes. Drum-major of *Regimiento de Zamora* in M1805 Uniform (right): The black coat had red collar, cuffs and lapels with white lacings. The bicorn has red, white and yellow plumes. A crimson and silver sash. Brown staff with silver knob.

M1805 Fusilier Uniform

The Royal Order of 15 April 1805 ordered that the infantry uniform once again changed back to white probably as an economy measure due to the scarcity of blue dye. The clothing was of good quality with the coat and waistcoat expected to last for thirty months, a shirt and a pair of breeches for fifteen months.

Finally when the Spanish soldiers in Northern Germany and Denmark in late 1807 to early 1808 received their M1805 uniforms, they were made in Paris and show some differences from the regulations due to the supply problems from far away Spain.

1807

Scharf after Christoph Suhr

Drim Major

Musicians

Musicians

Drum Major

Rgto de Princessa in M1802 uniform

Rgto de Zamora in M1805 uniform

HEADWEAR: Black felt bicorn with a red cockade and sometimes a red plume. White forage caps with facing colour piping and headband and regimental badge.

HAIR: Unpowdered hair and clean shaven.

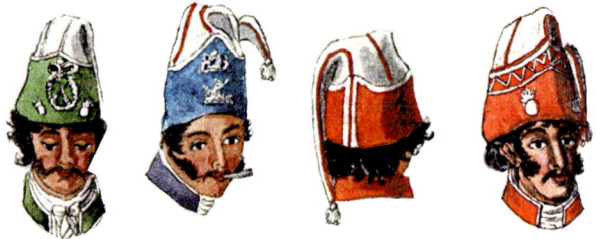

M1805

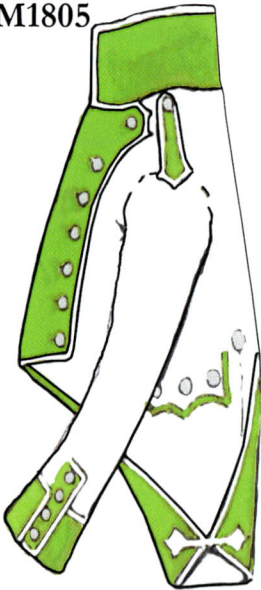

Fusilier Jacket

M1805 Fusilier bicorns and bonnet de police [Suhr]

COAT: White long tailed coat with facing colours shown on the collar, lapels, cuffs, cuff flaps, pocket flap edging, turnback piping and shoulder strap edging. A *fleur-de-lis* was on the collar. A heart shaped ornament in regimental colour was sewn onto the tips of the turnbacks.

BUTTONS: Each regiment bore its regimental title on its buttons.

WAISTCOAT: White waistcoat with sleeves laced with red laces.

LEGWEAR: White breeches with black knee length gaiters, long brown or checked trousers. Black shoes and often sandals were often worn.

DISTINCTIONS: NCOs wore fringed epaulettes in red but sometimes in facing colour. Officers had epaulettes in button colour, gilt gorget and scarlet sash. Drummers wore blue jacket with red facings.

EQUIPMENT: White belts.

SIDEARMS: Armed with muskets and bayonets. NCOs had grenadier sabres.

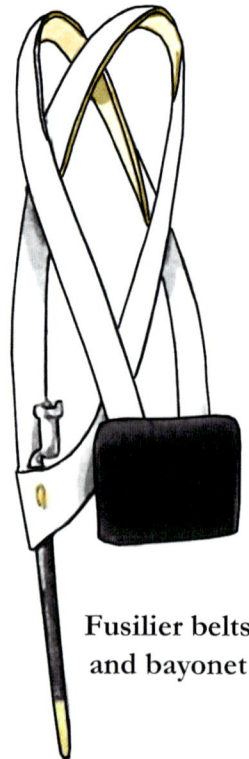

Fusilier belts and bayonet

Plate 5: Soldier of the *Regimiento de Guadalajara* leading a Spanish cart containing his family

By Christoph Suhr

This stalwart figure of the *Regimiento de Guadalajara* had the misfortune to be captured almost intact white trying to escape from Freyling. Happily 150 men from the *Regimientos de Asturias* and *de Guadalajara* managed to join the main body of troops under La Romana. This soldier wears his 1805 uniform and accompanies his whole family in rather a splendid Spanish wagon. A man of some means is indicated by the wagon being horse drawn.

Plate 6: Spanish infantrymen playing cards
By Christoph Suhr

The soldiers in great diversity of uniforms with close proximty of the precious beasts of burden are playing *l'Hombre* (also known as *Tresillo* (Spain), *Ombre* (Britain) and *Rocambor* (South America) a card game that dates from the 17th Century. Interestingly, *L'Hombre* is still played in Denmark especially in the areas of Jutland and Funen Island where La Romana Division were stationed. This was the first card game where the trump suit was established by bidding rather than by the random process of turning the first card of the deck and used 40 cards rather than the English 52 card deck.

Plate 7: Soldier leaving his comrades

By Christoph Suhr

This rather touching scene shows a Spanish infantryman wearing a brown greatcoat handing over a brandy bottle to his comrades in the Hamburg Militia as a parting gift. There is a contrast in colour between the seemingly dowdy brown greatcoat of the Spanish infantryman and the resplendent Hamburg Militia in their scarlet and sky blue uniforms. We are unable to tell which regiment the Spanish soldier hails from. Note his umbrella strapped to the top of his rather full knapsack.

M1805

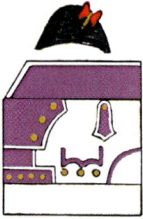
1st Rey

2nd Reina

3rd Príncipe

8th Soria

27th Princesa

4th Saboya

5th la Corona

6th Africa

9th Zamora

11th Sevilla

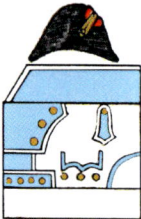
12th Granada

13th Valencia

16th Toledo

19th Murcia

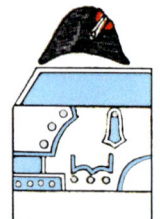
21st Cantabria

9th Córdoba

10th Guadalajara

17th Mallorca

20th León

25th Aragon

14th Zaragoza

15th España

18th Burgos

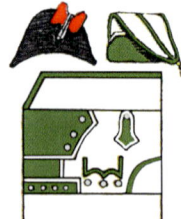
22nd Asturias

23rd Fijo
de Ceuta

Spanish M1805 Fusilier Uniform

M1805

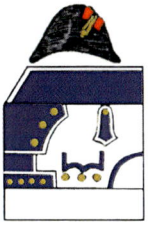

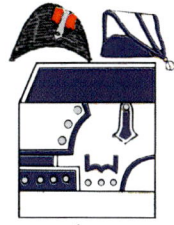

| 24th Navarra | 26th América | 29th Málaga | 30th Jaén | 31st Órdenes Militares |

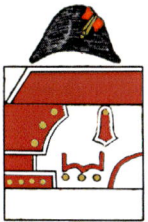
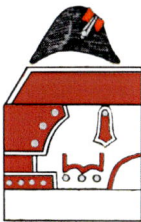

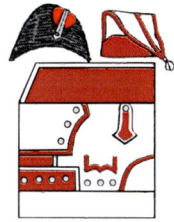

| 28th Extremadura | 32nd Castilla | 33rd Estado | 34th Corona | 35th Borbón |

Spanish M1805 Fusilier Uniform

Table 2: M1805 infantry facing colours

Brigade	Regiment	Cuffs and piping
White Coats		
1st	1° *Rey*, 2° *Reina*, 3° *Príncipe*, 8° *Soria*, 27° *Princesa*	Violet
2nd	4° *Saboya*, 5° *la Corona*, 6° *África*, 7° *Zamora*, 11° *Sevilla*	Black
3rd	12° *Granada*, 13° *Valencia*, 16° *Toledo*, 19° *Murcia*, 21° *Cantabria*	Light blue
4th	9° *Córdoba*, 10° *Guadalajara*, 17° *Mallorca*, 20° *León*, 25° *Aragón*	Scarlet
5th	14° *Zaragoza*, 15° *España*, 18° *Burgos*, 22° *Asturias*, 23° *Fijo de Ceuta*	Light green
6th	24° *Navarra*, 26° *América*, 29° *Málaga*, 30° *Jaén*, 31° *Órdenes Militares*	Dark blue
7th	28° *Extremadura*, 32° *Castilla*, 33° *Estado*, 34° *Corona*, 35° *Borbón*	Crimson
Light Blue Coats		
8th	36° *Irlanda*, 37° *Hibernia*, 38° *Ultonia*, 39° *Nápoles*	Yellow
Dark Blue Coats		
Swiss	1° *Wimpffen*, 2° *Reding*, 3° *Reding*, 4° *Betschartd*, 5° *Taxler*, 6° *Preux*	Red

1st Rey   2nd Reyna   3rd Príncipe   8th Soria   27th Princesa

1st Brigade (Violet) line infantry in M1805 uniform

Reglamento de Uniformidad del Ejército y la Marina en 1805

4th Saboya   5th la Corona   6th Africa   7th Zamora   11th Sevilla

2nd Brigade (Black) line infantry in M1805 uniform

Reglamento de Uniformidad del Ejército y la Marina en 1805

12th Granada   13th Valencia   16th Toledo   19th Murcia   21st Cantabria

3rd Brigade (Light Blue) line infantry in M1805 uniform

Reglamento de Uniformidad del Ejército y la Marina en 1805

9th Córdoba   10th Guadalajara   17th Mallorca   20th León   25th Aragon

4th Brigade (Scarlet) line infantry in M1805 uniform

Reglamento de Uniformidad del Ejército y la Marina en 1805

| 14th Zaragoza | 15th España | 18th Burgos | 22nd Asturias | 23rd Fijo de Ceuta |

5th Brigade (Light Green) line infantry in M1805 uniform

Reglamento de Uniformidad del Ejército y la Marina en 1805

| 24th Navarra | 26th América | 29th Málaga | 30th Jaén | 31st Órdenes Militares |

6th Brigade (Dark Blue) line infantry in M1805 uniform

Reglamento de Uniformidad del Ejército y la Marina en 1805

| 28th Extremadura | 32nd Castilla | 33rd Estado | 34th Corona | 35th Borbón |

7th Brigade (Crimson) line infantry in M1805 uniform

Reglamento de Uniformidad del Ejército y la Marina en 1805

Spanish Grenadiers on Parade for Marshal Bernadotte

After Christoph Suhr by Richard Knotel

Spanish Grenadiers
[Bradford, 1809]

Left is the rear view of a grenadier of the *Rgto de Estamadura* and
right is the side view of a *Rgto de Zaragoza* in M1805 uniform.

Grenadier Uniforms

In garrison, the Grenadier companies were normally excused the policing and mounting patrols of towns that the centre fusilier companies were employed in. Instead, the grenadiers would be called upon to provide the guards at the doors of the residence of generals. The lesser officers would merit fusiliers.

HEADWEAR: Bearskin grenadier cap. The grenadier silk flamers were in regimental facing colour. Prior to 1805, all flamers were scarlet.

TUNIC. White coat with regimental facings and grenade badge on the turnbacks. Grenadiers had shoulder straps in facing colour edged white with tufts in facing colour and white. The cuffs had white vertical bars.

Sergeant (left) and Grenadier (right) M1805 uniform

Match case

DISTINCTIONS: NCOs had fringed epaulettes in facing colour and single stripe on sleeve.

LEGWEAR: White breeches, black gaiters and shoes.

EQUIPMENT: The brass match case for a length of smouldering "slow match" was worn on the cross belt and was the relic from the days when grenadiers threw hand grenades.

Grenadier equipment

White leather belts, cartridge box, sabre and bayonet

Spanish Grenadier caps and flames
By Christoph Suhr

Plate 8: Grenadiers and Pioneers of the *Rgtos de la Princesa, Zamora,* and *Guadalajara*
By Christoph Suhr

This Plate from Suhr (1808) depicts an elite grouping of three grenadiers and two pioneers all proudly in full dress. The mixture of uniforms is readily apparent with, for example, the two grenadiers of the *Rgto de Zamora* wearing both the 1802 and 1805 uniforms. The main reason for this being the older uniforms were worn out first due in the main to a shortage of funds in most infantry and cavalry regiments because of Godoy's interference and mismanagement in military matters pertaining to uniform issuance, not to mention appropriation of funds destined for the line troops.

The heavily embroidered flames on the backs of the bearskins are remarkable in their intricacy and sheer vibrancy of colour. In fact the base colour of the flame was in the appropriate facing colour of the regiment with its own distinctive pattern. The two grenadiers of the *Rgto de Zamora* stand out as both wear the old and new uniforms for added variety of colour.

Grenadier of *Rgto de la Princesa* in the new M1805 Uniform (Left)
Pioneer of the *Rgto de Zamora* in M1802 Uniform (Centre left)
Pioneer of the *Rgto de Guadalajara* in the M1805 Uniform (Centre)
Grenadier of the *Rgto de Zamora* in M1802 Uniform (Centre right)
Grenadier of the *Rgto de Zamora* in the new M1805 Uniform (Right)

Regimiento de Guadalajara in Hamburg, c1807
[After Weber]

Plate 9: Grenadiers of the *Regimiento de Guadalajara*
By Christoph Suhr

The Grenadiers were a firm favourite of Christoph Suhr in his life sketches. Resplendent in their unusually tall black bearskins the elite troops of La Romana Division were the Grenadiers. Alongside the resilient artillerymen, these were the cream of the fighting forces of Spain despite their outdated appearance. The brass pouch grenade and brass match case show the origins of these soldiers who up to the middle of the 18th century used grenades. The intricate hand stitched scarlet flame with white lace decoration and tassel can be clearly seen on the back of the Sergeant of the *Rgto de Guadalajara* (indicated by his scarlet rank stripe) addressing his Grenadiers. The circular patch at the top bears the figure of St George on a grey charger on a light blue ground. The scarlet facings of the Grenadiers contrast well with the heavy duty M1805 white woollen uniforms. Note the clear depiction of the M1801 brass mounted muskets. The white lace on the cuffs surmounted with stamped pewter buttons completes the picture.

Grenadiers of the Rgto de Zamora
[Weber, 1807]

Plate 10: Guard of honour for Marshal Bernadotte
By Christoph Suhr

Christoph Suhr depicts the guard of honour formed by the grenadiers of *Regimiento de Zamora* for Marshal Bernadotte. The grenadiers were chosen for their size, strength and intelligence. The grenadier company of the *Regimiento de Zamora* in full dress is a striking example of the pinnacle of elegance reached by the Spanish infantry in 1808. This was noted by Marshal Bernadotte at the time.

Not visible in the figures depicted but a distinguishing mark is the black cartouche box adorned with a brass grenade, a symbol of their elite status, not to mention the elegant but unadorned black bearskins devoid of the customary scarlet plume. In this interesting plate the captain talks to his fellow officer of the *1° Cazadores de Cataluña Bn* while the Regimental drummer of *Rgto de Zamora*, dressed in dark blue coat and red facings edged white, awaits the instructions from the officers.

Grenadier of Rgto de Zamora, c1807
[Scharf after Suhr]

Plate 11: Grenadiers of the *Rgto de Zamora* under an umbrella
By Christoph Suhr

Two Spanish Grenadiers from the *Rgto de Zamora* in undress uniform sheltering from the Hamburg rain. The distinctive black cuffs and white collar of this regiment being plainly visible. Umbrellas were favoured by all ranks of La Romana Division without distinction unlike the British Army where only officers sported this sensible piece of kit. The figure on the right has no pressed steel grenade badge on his *bonnet-de-police* but makes up for this with his crimson sash.

Pioneer Uniforms

The pioneer uniform varied considerably from regiment to regiment. Aprons varied from brown to buff. Their headwear consisted of a large bearskin with a grenadier bag and a large brass or white metal plate with various crests. Beards and moustaches were compulsory.[118]

Vaughan Funnell

Sapper

Plate 12: Pioneer and grenadiers of *Regimiento de Zamora*
By Christoph Suhr

The pioneer is wearing a black fur bearskin cap which had an oversized brass plate, red plume and black flame with white piping, black facings and red collar. He carries the tools of his trade: black leather apron and trenching tools in the form of a spade. All three figures have scalloped edged epaulettes without fringes that were common in most other countries for these elite troops. The sabre and bayonet sheaths are black leather with brass fittings. Light blue and white chequered trousers.

The grenadier in the centre has a black bicorn hung off his goatskin pack. The light blue and white chequered trousers are really civilian dress worn by the troops in lieu of the white woollen full dress breeches. They are cut more like pantaloons and so must have been comfortable and practical to wear.

The figure on the right is certainly a grenadier despite wearing a black bicorn with red cockade and plume of a centre company because he has a grenadier sabre and a brass match case on his cross-belts.

---

[118] Elting (2000) II: Plate 116 and Nafziger (1992) p25

Plate 13: Grenadiers and pioneers of *Rgtos de Zamora* and *de Guadalajara*

By Christoph Suhr

Another fascinating grouping of the Elite companies of the *Regimientos de Zamora* and *Guadalajara*. Of particular interest is the hanging bag of figure three, the pioneer of the Zamora regiment, as it appears that the Spanish pioneer bag decorations were of a simpler nature then those worn by their comrades in the Grenadier companies.

Also of note are the variable entrenching tools carried, in this plate a hefty entrenching axe. Also visible are the crimson and white tassels worn on the black leather apron and the full beards sported by the two sappers/pioneers depicted. The figure second from the right has what appears to be a white linen dust coat normally worn in the heat of Spain, complete with steel buttons. The wearing of scarlet plumes by grenadiers and sappers seems to have been arbitrary.

(1 & 2) Front and rear view of a Grenadier of the *Regimiento de Zamora*. Violet facings, white buttons and red bonnet flames with yellow lace. Brass pouch badge and sabre fittings.

(3) Rear view of a Pioneer of *Regimiento de Zamora*. Black facings, epaulettes and cap flame. White lace to bonnet flame. Circular light blue patch with arm holding the Spanish flag. Brass cap plate, pouch badge and sabre fittings. Red plume.

Pioneer of Rgto de la Princesa in M1802 uniform

(4) Grenadier of *Regimiento de Guadalajara* in greatcoat. Red plume and white buttons.

(5) Pioneer of *Regimiento de Guadalajara*. Red facings and bonnet flame. White buttons, decoration to the flame. Circular patch at the top. Brass cap plate and match case. Black leather apron with white and red tassels. Red epaulettes.

Spanish pioneer
bearskin caps
[Suhr]

Plate 14: Pioneers of *Rgtos de la Princesa* and *de Asturias*

By Christoph Suhr

Left: a pioneer of the *Rgto de la Princesa* in M1802 uniform (left) wearing a black bearskin colpack with a brass plate and red bag with white tassel. Light blue jacket with black facings edged red, yellow buttons and collar badge. The black apron had buff leather pockets for nails adorned with white and red tassels.

Centre: a pioneer of the *Rgto de la Princesa* in M1805 uniform wears the M1805 uniform but has light blue rather than violet facings.

Right: a pioneer of the *Rgto de Asturias* in M1805 uniform has a white jacket with light green cuffs, light green lapels and white collar piped light green, white buttons. The black bearskin cap has a white metal cap plate with brass emblems and light green bag. The light brown leather apron is edged with light green and has a light green grenade in the centre. Black gaiters and black shoes.

Chapter 4
Line Infantry Uniforms in May 1808

As has been already stated the uniforms of the infantry were a mixture of the 1802 and 1805 patterns as identified by Sorando Muzás (2012) through his research in the archives of the eve of the Peninsular War. Two wore the M1797 uniform, twelve the M1802 uniform and only the remaining twenty-one wore the M1805 uniform as noted in Table 3.

Table 3: Infantry Uniform on 28 April 1808 [Sorando Muzás (2012)]

Regiment	Uniform Notes
Rgto de África	**Blue M1802 uniform** was issued on 13 March 1803. **White M1805 uniform** by April 1808. General Castaños dressed in this uniform for the majority of his life in recognition of his grenadiers who rescued him during the Roussillon Campaign.
Rgto de América	**White M1805 uniform** by March 1808.
Rgto de Aragón	**Blue M1802 uniform** was issued at the start of 1803.
Rgto de Asturias	**White M1805 uniform** in 1807.
Rgto de Borbón	**White M1805 uniform** by March 1808.
Rgto de Burgos	**White M1805 uniform** by March 1808.
Rgto de Cantabria	**White M1805 uniform** by March 1808.
Vol. de Castilla	**Blue M1802 uniform** was issued in October 1804. **White M1805 uniform.** Issued in Oct 1808 by the Junta of Valencia.
Rgto de Córdoba	**White M1805 uniform** by March 1808.
Rgto de la Corona	**Blue M1802 uniform** was issued in August 1804.
Vol. de la Corona	**Blue M1802 uniform** was issued in January 1804.
Rgto de España	**Blue M1802 uniform** was issued in August 1803.
Vol. del Estado	**Blue M1802 uniform** was issued on 1 December 1805 but was disbanded before it could get its new uniform. Their **White M1805 uniform** with crimson facings was issued to the new *1° Rgto de Voluntarios de Madrid*.
Rgto de Extremadura	**Blue M1802 uniform** was issued in February 1805. In Saragossa (June-Aug 1808), the regiment received 1000 jackets of unknown colour, 704 trousers, 444 shirts and 570 hats, as well as 600 ponchos, 300 shirts and an indeterminate number of cartridge belts. In November after the retreat from Tudela, the regiment still had 197 jackets and 435 ponchos of the M1802 pattern. On 2 Dec 1808, awarded the *Defensor de Zaragoza* embroidered in their left sleeve.

Regiment	Uniform Notes
Rgto Fijo de Ceuta	**White M1797 uniform** with green facings was issued in October 1801.
Rgto de Granada	**Blue M1802 uniform** was issued in May 1804.
Rgto de Guadalajara	**White M1805 uniform** was issued to II Bn (1 July 1806) and I & III Bns (2 Mar 1807). This was made in Paris so diverged slightly from the official pattern.
Rgto de Jaén	**White M1797 uniform** with red collar and lapels, black turnbacks and white buttons was issued in April 1802. This white M1797 uniform was still worn on 29 Mar 1808. Some of its officers by May 1808 wore the M1805 uniform as shown in a portrait of his Captain A. Aguado.
Rgto de León	**Blue M1802 uniform** was issued at the start of 1804. From Sept 1808, the III Bn wore a brown jacket, waistcoat and trousers.
Rgto de Málaga	**White M1797 uniform** was issued in August 1799.
Rgto de Mallorca	**White M1805 uniform** by March 1808.
Rgto de Murcia	**White M1805 uniform** by March 1808.
Rgto de Navarra	**White M1805 uniform** by March 1808.
Rgto de Órdenes Militares	**White M1805 uniform** by March 1808.
Rgto de la Princesa	**Blue M1802 inform** in c1804. **White M1805 uniform** was worn from 1 Jan 1808-Apr 1810. This was made in Paris so diverged slightly from the official pattern.
Rgto del Príncipe	**White M1805 uniform** was issued in July 1807.
Rgto del Rey	**Blue M1802 uniform** was issued in September 1803.
Rgto de la Reina	**Blue M1802 uniform** was issued in January 1804. These were supplemented from 26 Oct 1808 by 500 jackets from *Rgto de Irlanda*. **New jackets** issued in Jan 1809 were white with red facings.
Rgto de Saboya	**White M1805 uniform** by March 1808.
Rgto de Sevilla	Blue M1802 uniform was issued in June 1803. **White M1805 uniform** in March 1808.
Rgto de Soria	**White M1805 uniform** by March 1808.
Rgto de Toledo	**White M1805 uniform** by March 1808.
Rgto de Valencia	**White M1805 uniform** by March 1808.
Rgto de Zamora	**White M1805 uniform** in May 1807 made in Paris so diverged slightly from the official pattern. **New uniform** was issued on 8 October 1808.
Rgto de Zaragoza	**Blue M1802 uniform** was issued in June 1803. **Red Canadian militia jackets** (Aug 1808) were issued to the I & II Bns.

Summerfield, 2013

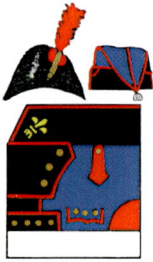 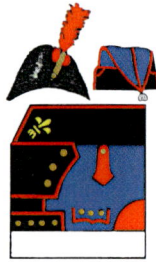   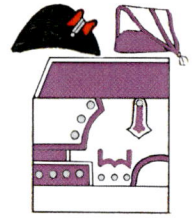

1st Rey   2nd Reina   3rd Principe   8th Soria   27th Princesa

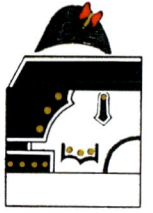 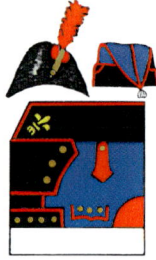   

4th Saboya   5th la Corona   6th Africa   9th Zamora   11th Sevilla

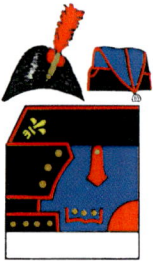 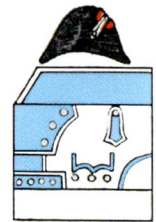   

12th Granada   13th Valencia   16th Toledo   19th Murcia   21st Cantabria

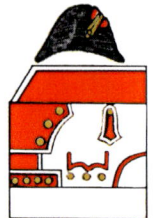 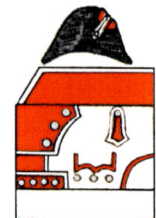   

9th Cordoba   10th Guadalajara   17th Mallorca   20th Leon   25th Aragon

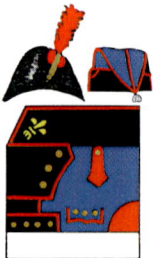 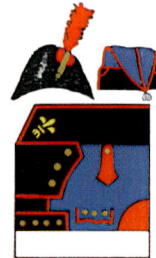  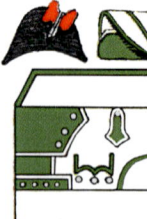 

14th Zaragoza   15th Espana   18th Burgos   22nd Asturias   23rd Fijo de Ceuta (M1797)

Fusilier uniforms on 28 April 1808
according to Sorando Muzás (2012)

~ 104 ~

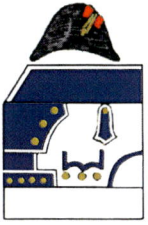

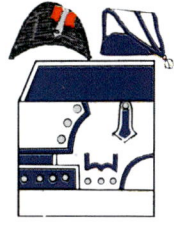

| 24th Navarra | 26th America | 29th Malaga (M1797) | 30th Jaen | 31st Ordenes Militares |

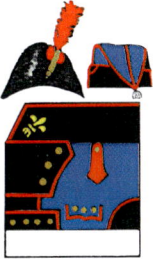
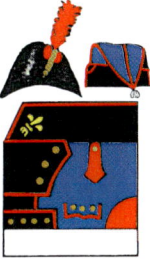
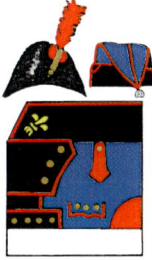
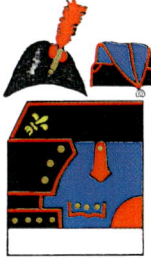

| 28th Estremadur | 32nd Castilla | 33rd Estado | 34th Corona | 35th Borbon |

Fusilier uniforms on 28 April 1808
according to Sorando Muzás (2012)

New Regiments

The Bourbon Army fought well in 1808 and was not the same army that fought the rest of the Peninsular War. Cadres of old soldiers were used as the local juntas recruited their own armies by adopting any surviving regulars and raising new "volunteer" units. The lack of horses in Spain meant most of these new units were infantry. Even universities contributed staff and students to the cause.

The following illustrations are based upon reconstructions by Jose Bueno and show the complexity of the myriad of uniforms and units formed in 1808-09. Many were uniformed in the inexpensive brown cloth.

The *Voluntarios de la Defensa de Barcelona* were raised on 10 October 1808 for the defence of the city of Barcelona during the siege (1 Aug – 17 Dec 1808).

1808

Voluntarios de la Defensa de Barcelona
After Bueno

1809

Batallon de Voluntarios
Almogavares

The Bn de Vol de Almogares was formed in 1809 as a body of men and horsemen armed with a variety of weapons including halberds, axes, javelins and blunderbuses.

1808

Cadetes de Sevilla

1809

Fusiler

Rgto Infanteria de Baza
By Beaufort

Soldier

Officer

Voluntarios Vizcaino
By Bueno

The Catalonia and the Basque country had a tradition of local armed irregulars (the *migueletes* and *somatenes*). The name derives from Miguelot de Prats who was a Catalan mercenary captain in the service of Cesare Borgia. They were raised at the parish level and would turn out for duty on the sound of the village alarm-bell (*someten*) so were also known as *somatenes*.

1809

Miguelete

Provisional
de la Victoria

**Migueletes de la
Nouvelle Castille**

1809

Escuadras de Valls

Patriotas Coy   Minones de Valencia

1808

Voluntarios
de Infanteria
de Navarra

1809

José Mª Bueno

Miñónes de Alava

Corregimentos
de Cerezo

1808

Santa
Hermandad

Fusileros
de Aragon José Mª Bueno

By 1809 there were over 100 new infantry regiments contributing at least 150 new battalions. Many regiments had a short lifespan due to lack of supplies and the losses suffered in many battles and sieges. Many changed their names or were amalgamated with other units and some were even re-raised. The uniforms worn by these new formations would require considerable more research and are outside the scope of this book.

Chapter 5
Foreign Infantry Regiments

Traditionally, the Spanish army comprised a relatively large number of foreign regiments but difficulties in recruiting meant that in 1792, four foreign regiments (*Milán, Flandes, Brabante* and *Bruselas*) were disbanded and those that remained were seriously understrength.

Italian Regiments
Rgto de Nápoles

In 1572, *Tercio Viejo de la Armada del Mar Océano de Infantería Napolitana* was raised by Don Lelio Grissoni in the Bourbon Kingdom of Naples. In 1707, the regiment was renamed *Rgto de Nápoles*. On 22 March 1792, *Rgtos de Milán* and *de Flanders* were absorbed by the regiment. In 1809, the regiment was absorbed into the *Rgto del Rey*. The reformed regiment absorbed the *Cazadores del Campo de Cariñena* (Est. 1 May 1809) and *Rgto Provisional de Cansados de Galicia* (Est. 1 Oct 1811) on 2 March 1815.

Rgto de Nápoles, c1806
Reglamento de Uniformidad del Ejercito y la Marina en 1805

Campaign History: In 1784-90, the regiment was the garrison of San Juan in Puerto Rico. During the 1793-95 Roussillon Campaign the regiment was distinguished at Castel-Pignon and Valcarlos. From 1805, recruits could not be obtained from the Kingdom of Naples so the *Regimiento de Nápoles* was reduced to a weak half-strength combined battalion. In May 1808, the Combined Bn in Ferrol in Galicia had only 288 men. In June, it was part of the Army of Galicia. Fought at Valmaseda (5 Nov) and Espinosa (10-11 Nov). Almost destroyed at Mansilla de las Mulas (30 Dec).

Flag - The flags of the *Regimiento de Nápoles* had a sky blue shield with a black horse. The flags of *Regimiento de Milán* were white with a green snake devouring a child.

Flag of Rgto de Milan (1768-1805)

Irish Regiments

The Irish regiments, formed from Irishmen seeking to practice their religion freely and to fight the British, were transferred from French service on 1 November 1709 (*Regimientos de Hibernia, de Ultonia* and *de Irlanda*). Unfortunately the number of Irish declined and the quality of these regiments fell dramatically. As a result the foreign regiments were severely under strength with the *Regimiento de Ultonia* having only enough men for a single half-strength combined battalion.

Traditionally the Irish regiments had red coats. This changed in 1802 to white and then to sky blue in 1805. The flags of the three Irish Regiments (*Regimientos de Hibernia, Ultonia* and *Irlanda*) bore the Irish harp in the corner devices of both the *Coronela* and *Sencilla*.

Officer of Rgto de Irlanda
[Goddard and Booth, 1809]

Rgto de Hibernia

In 1709, *Rgto de Castelar* was formed by Coronel D. Lucas Patiño Marqués de Castelar from Irishmen in Spanish service. On 28 November 1791, *Rgto de Brabante* was absorbed by *Rgto de Hibernia*. The *Reunion de Aragón* (Est. 20 July 1808), *2º Rgto de Guadalajara* (27 Dec 1811) and *Rgto de la Constitución* (Est. 15 Apr 1812) were absorbed on 2 March 1815. On 1 June 1818, the regiment was dissolved and absorbed by *Rgtos de Zamora, Mallorca* and *Jaén*.

Campaign History: In 1762, the regiment participated in the war with Portugal. In 1775, the regiment was part of the invasion of Algiers (1775), based in Cuba with detachments in Louisiana (1776). In the Louisiana and Western Florida Campaigns (1777-81) captured Fort Bute (7 Sept 1779), Baton Rouge and Fort Panmure at Natchez (13 Sept 1779), Fort Charlotte at Mobile (1-14 Mar 1780) and Pensacola (9 Mar-8 May 1781) and was stationed in Santo Domingo for the abortive invasion of Jamaica (1782).

Participated in the war in Africa (1791), Roussillon Campaign (1793-95), war against Portugal (1800-02). In May 1808, the regiment totalled only 854 men with the I Bn in Asturias and the II & III Bns in Ferrol in Galicia. In June, the regiment joined the Army of Galicia. The II & III Bns fought at Medina de Rioseco while I Bn was in the Asturias and later fought at Zornoza (30 Oct).

Shield - Blue with a harp, and the

Rgto de Hibernia
(Est. 1709)

motto *IN HOMNEN TERRAM EXHIVIT SONUS EORUM*.[119]

Rgto de Hibernia, c1806
Reglamento de Uniformidad del Ejercito y la Marina en 1805

Coronela

Sencilla

Rgto de Hibernia

---

[119] *Coronela* of *Regimiento de Hibernia* - Reg. No. 21097 (1790-1809) and 41205 (1810-18) [Sorando Muzás (2000) pp185 & 187]

Rgto de Irlanda

Formed in 1688 as the *Regiment de las Guardias de la Reina de Inglaterra* in French service. In 1709, *Rgto de Wachop* under *Coronel* D. Francisco Wachop entered Spanish service. On 1 June 1818, dissolved and absorbed by *Rgtos des Rey, de Asturias* and *de la Princesa*.

Campaign History: War with Portugal (1762). Garrison of Cuba (1771). Invasion of Algiers (1775). Based in Cuba with detachments in Louisiana (1776-81), captured Fort Bute (7 Sept 1779), Baton Rouge and Fort Panmure at Natchez (13 Sept 1779), Fort Charlotte at Mobile (1-14 Mar 1780) and Pensacola (9 Mar-8 May 1781). War in Africa (1789-91). Roussillon Campaign (1793-95). In May 1808, I Bn was in Olivenza and the II-III Bns in Puerto de Santa María in Andalucía (513 men). Joined the Army of Andalusia. The II and III Bn fought at battle of Medina de Rioseco while I Bn was in the Asturias. I Bn was almost destroyed at Uclés (13 Jan 1809). Fought at Medellín (29 Mar 1809).

Rgto de Irlanda, c1806

Reglamento de Uniformidad del Ejercito y la Marina en 1805

Regimento de Irlanda

Coronela [Colonel's] *Flag*

Ordenanza Flag

Shield - Blue with a harp with the motto below of *IN HOMNEN TERRAM EXHIVIT SONUS EORUM*.[120]

---

[120] *Coronela* of *Regimiento de Irlanda* - Reg No. 21248 (1810-18) [Sorando Muzás (2000) p187]

Rgto de Ultonia

In 1709, *Rgto de MacAulif* was formed from Irish émigrés by Coronel D. Demetrio MacAulif. In 1718, the regiment was renamed *Rgto de Infantería Fijo de Ultonia*. Absorbed *Rgto de Alpujarras* (Est. 14 June 1808) and *Rgto de Leales Manresanos* (Est. 7 Sept 1811) on 2 March 1815. On 1 June 1818, the regiment was dissolved.

Campaign History: War with Portugal (1762). Garrison in Cuba with detachments in Louisiana (1769) and Mexico City in New Spain (1770-71). Participated in the capture of Fort Bute (7 Sept 1779), Baton Rouge and Fort Panmure at Natchez (13 Sept 1779), siege of Savannah (23 Sept-20 Oct 1779), siege and capture of Fort Charlotte at Mobile (1-14 March 1780), Siege and Capture of Pensacola (9 Mar-8 May 1781) and reconquest of Mahón (1781-83).

War in Africa (1789-91) and Roussillon Campaign (1793-95). In May 1808, the Combined Bn was in Gerona, Catalonia (351 men). The regiment joined the Army of Catalonia and fought at the defence of Gerona (20 June 1808), the defence of Rosas (7 Nov-5 Dec 1808) and the defence of Gerona (6 June-10 Dec 1809).

Rgto de Ultonia, c1806
Reglamento de Uniformidad del Ejercito y la Marina en 1805

Rgto de Ultonia
(Est. 1709)

Shield - Blue with a harp and ducal crown and the motto *"IN HOMNEN TERRAM EXHIBIT SONUS EORUM."* Added were the battle honours to commemorate the battle of *"CAMPO SANTO"* in Italy (1743) and *"BIDASSOA"* granted in 1794 by Carlos IV.[121]

---

[121] *Coronela* of *Regimiento de Ultonia* - Reg. No. 21084 (1810-18) [Sorando Muzás (2000) p187]

M1805 Uniform

HEADWEAR: Black bicorn with large red cockade. Grenadiers wore the tall black bearskin cap with long heavily embroidered triangular bag in regimental facing colour with tassel.

COAT: Light blue coat and turnbacks with yellow piping. Light blue waistcoat.

DISTINCTIONS: Officers had epaulettes in button colour and scarlet sash.

LEGWEAR: Light blue breeches with black gaiters. Breeches were often replaced by long brown or checked trousers. Black shoes.

Rgto de Napoles

Note the artist has not shown the highly embroidered flame.

Table 4: M1805 Foreign Regiments uniform

	Collar	cuffs & turnbacks	lapels	buttons
36° Irlanda	Yellow piped white	Yellow	Yellow piped white	Brass
37° Hibernia	Sky blue piped yellow	Yellow	Yellow piped white	White metal
38° Nápoles	Yellow piped white	Yellow	Sky blue piped white	White metal
39° Ultonia	Yellow piped white	Yellow	Yellow piped white	White metal

M1805   Irish Regiments   Italian Regiment

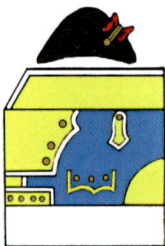

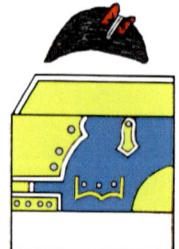

36th Irlanda   37th Hibernia   38th Ultonia   39th Nápoles

Foreign Regiments
[Summerfield, 2013]

~ 114 ~

Chapter 6
Swiss Regiments

The Swiss regiments were known by the name of the colonel of the regiment. Unlike the line infantry each Swiss regiment had two battalions, each comprising six companies of 200 men. Only Catholics were admitted into these Swiss regiments. The decline in numbers was less severe in the Swiss Infantry Regiment but their national character declined with time as less Swiss were in their ranks.

I Bn command:

1 *coronel* (colonel), 1 *sargento mayor* (major), 1 *ayudante* (adjutant), 1 *abanderado* (standard-bearer), 2 *subtenientes* (supernumerary 2nd lt), 7 *gastadores* (pioneer/ sappers), 1 *tambor mayor* (drum-major), 2 *pífanos* (fifers), 1 *preboste* (provost), 1 *maestro armero* (master armourer), 1 *capellán* (chaplain), 1 *cirujano* (surgeon), 1 *cura* (clerk).

II Bn command:

1 *teniente coronel* (colonel), 1 *ayudante* (adjutant), 1 *abanderado* (standard-bearer), 2 *subtenientes* (2nd lt), 7 *gastadores* (pioneers/sappers), 2 *pífanos* (fifers), 1 *preboste* (provost), 1 *maestro armero* (master armourer), 1 *capellán* (chaplain), 1 *cirujano* (surgeon].

Grenadier Company:

1 *capitán* (captain), 1 *teniente* (1st lt), 1 *subteniente* (2nd lt), 1 *sargento primero* (1st sergeant), 2 *sargentos segundos* (2nd sergeants), 4 *cabos primeros* (corporals), 4 *cabos segundos* (lance corporals), 2 *tambores* (drummers), 96 *granaderos* (grenadiers).

Fusilier Company:

1 *capitán primero* (1st captain), 1 *capitán secundo* (2nd captain), 2 *teniente* (1st lt), 2 *subteniente* (2nd lt), 1 *sargento primero* (1st sergeant), 5 *sargentos segundos* (2nd sergeant), 8 *cabos primeros* (corporals), 8 *cabos segundos* (lance corporals), 4 *tambores* (drummers), 174 *fusileros* (fusiliers).

In May 1808, the *2º Rgto Suizo de Reding* (also known as *de Ruttiman*) and *6º Rgto Suizo de Preux* were pressed into French service and were present at Bailén (19 July 1808) when they deserted back to their Spanish masters.

Swiss Regimental Flags

From at least 1732 the *Coronela* had royal arms like those of the Spanish Infantry and the *Sencilla* had the arms of their Colonel (Chef) and probably flames arising from the intersection of the red Cross of Burgundy and spreading towards the margins of the cloth.[122] In 1749, the regulations reduced the *Rgtos Suizos* from three battalions to two where each company carried a flag. The white *Coronela* carried by the 1st company of I battalion and the *Sencilla* of the other companies was in the facing colour of the regiment with the Cross of Burgundy and in the corners pennants of the colour of the respective cantons. In c1760, the number of flags was reduced to two per battalion. The white *Coronela* with the royal arms,[123] was carried by the I Bn. The *Sencilla* had variations upon the design given. The flags were not always renewed after the change of Colonel. Interestingly at Bailén (19 July 1808), the *2° Rgto Suizo de Reding* and *6° Rgto Suizo de Preux* who were impressed into French service still carried the two Sencilla flags that they had used in the service of Carlos IV of Spain.

Swiss Infantry Regiments
1° Rgto Suizo

This was the oldes of the Swiss Regiments formed in 1734 in the Canton of Solothurn by Don Felix Jeronimo de Sury of Steinbruk.

Colonel in Chief
1734: *José de Sury de Steimbruk*
1745: *Félix Jerónimo de Buch*
1781: Vacant
1784: *Adams Krytter*
1790: *Francisco José de Schwaller*
1803: *António Schmid*
1805-35: *Luís Von Wimpffen*

Campaign History: In May 1808, the I-II Bns were in Tarragona (2,079 men). Joined the Army of Catalonia and at the defence of Rosas (7 Nov-5 Dec). In 1809, fought at Valls (25 Feb).

Flags - *Suizo de Schwaller* (1790-1802). Blue field with a red Cross of Burgundy with the coat of arms of Schwaller of a horse rampant white horse and ducal crown.[124]

1° Suizo de Wimpffen, 1805
Reglamento de Uniformidad del Ejército y la Marina en 1805

---

[122] Sorando Muzás (2000) p69.
[123] Reg. No. 21285 (1809-10) [Sorando Muzás (2000) p185]
[124] A very deteriorated example is at the Museum of History in Barcelona. [Sorando Muzás (2000) p69 and Note 262 p160]

2º Suizo de Reding, 1805
Reglamento de Uniformidad del Ejército y la Marina en 1805

2° Rgto Suizo

Formed in 1743 in the Swiss Canton of Schwyz. In 1810, dissolved and incorporated into *1°* and *4° Rgto Suizos*. The regiment was either known as Reding senior or Ruttiman after its commander, Cristóbal de Ruttiman.

Colonel in Chief
1742: *D. Jorge Dhumant*
1773: *D. José Fidel Barón de Thurn*
1792-1810: *Theodor Reding*

Campaign History: In May 1808, both Bns were in Talavera de la Reina, New Castile with 1,573 men. In June 1808, it was impressed into French service and fought against the Spanish at Alcolea (6 June). It was captured at Bailén (19 July) and most chose to serve in the Spanish Army. In 1809, it fought at Valls (25 Feb) and was disbanded in 1810.

Flag - *Suizo de Reding* (1792-1810) carried a *Sencilla* made up of yellow, blue and white alternate flames, a red cross with a deer at its intersection and the Ruttiman shield in each corner.[125]

2° Suizo de Reding (1792-1810)

Coronela Flag

Sencilla Flag

---

[125] Reg. No. 40829 (1798-1808) [Sorando Muzás (2000) p185]

3° Rgto Suizo

It was formed in 1743 in the Swiss Canton of Schwyz. Dissolved in 1829.

Colonel in Chief

1742: *D. José Carlos Barón de Reding de Biberregg*
1763: *D. Carlos Barón de Reding de Biberregg*
1780: *D. Antônio Barón de Reding de Biberregg*
1781: *D. Carlos Ehrler*
1789: *D. Teodoro Barón de Reding de Biberregg*
1807: *D. Nazario de Reding de Biberregg* (Reding Junior)
1815: *D. Antônio Kayser*
1819: Vacant
1829: Disbanded

Campaign History: In 1794, the *Rgto Suizo de Reding* received the shield of distinction for the battle Irún[263]. In May 1808, the I-II Bns were in Málaga (1,809 men). Joined the Army of Andalusia that fought at Alcolea (7 June) and Bailén (19 July).

Flag - *Suizo de Reding Junior* (1792-1808) carried a *Sencilla* made up of yellow, blue and white alternate flames, a red cross with a deer at its intersection and the Redding shield in each corner.[126]

3° Suizo de Reding Junior
Reglamento de Uniformidad del Ejército y la Marina en 1805

---

[126] Reg. No. 40829 (1798-1808) [Sorando Muzás (2000) p185]

4º Rgto Suizo

Formed in 1743 and dissolved in 1823.

Colonel in Chief

1743: *José Carlos Barón de Reding de Biberregg*
1751: *José Ultrich de Reding de Biberregg*
1757: *Carlos José Barón de Reding de Biberregg*
1761: *Luís Barón de Reding de Biberregg*
1768: *Carlos Janser*
1769: *Francisco Teodoro de Betschartd*
1798: *Domingo de Betschartd*
1815: *Francisco Zey*
1823: Disbanded

Campaign History: In May 1808, the I-II Bns were in Mallorca (2,051 men) when it joined the Army of Catalonia.

Flag - *Suizo de Betschartd* carried a large flag measuring 210cm by 230cm. The red field had a white Maltese Cross and four narrow white flames from under the centre of the cross. In the canton, on the white flame was a small portrait of the Madonna and Child sitting on a throne.[127]

4º Suizo de Betschartd, 1805
Reglamento de Uniformidad del Ejercito y la Marina en 1805

4º Suizo de Betschartd (1761-1823)

Coronela Flag

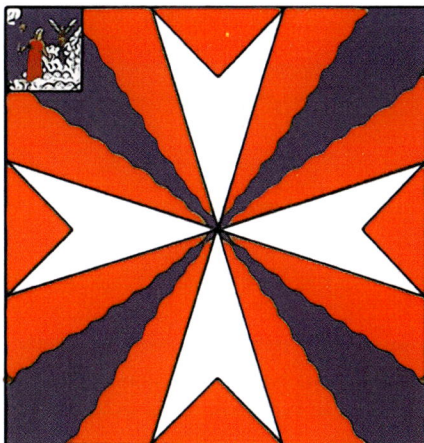

Sencilla Flag

---

[127] Wise (1978) III-30. These are preserved at the Museum of History in Bern and the National Museum in Zurich. [Sorando Muzás (2000) p69 and Note 259 on p160]

5° Rgto Suizo

This regiment was hired on 2 September 1793 and it was only approved on 1 October 1796. In 1810, dissolved and incorporated into *3° Rgto Suizo*.

Colonel in Chief
1794: *D. Carlos Yann*
1805-10: *D. Jorge Traxler* (or *Traschler*)

Campaign History: May 1808: I-II Bns were in Cartagena with 1,757 men as part of the Army of Valencia. Half of I Bn was captured at Rio Cabriel (14 June) and were taken into King Joseph's service only to desert at the first opportunity. In 1809, a half Bn fought at Alcañiz (23 May) and Belchite (18 June).

5° Suizo de Traxler, 1805
Reglamento de Uniformidad del Ejercito y la Marina en 1805

6° Rgto Suizo

Formed on 18 October 1796 in the Republic of Valais. On 22 September 1805, the King of Spain hired the regiment from the Republic of Valais so the regiment was not Swiss. In 1810, dissolved and incorporated into *1°* and *4° Rgto Suizos*.

6° Suizo de Courten, 1805
Reglamento de Uniformidad del Ejercito y la Marina en 1805

Colonel in Chief

1796: *D. Juan António de Courten.*
1803: *D. Elías de Courten.*
1808: *D. Carlos de Preux*
1810: Dissolved

Campaign History: In May 1808, I-II Bns were in Madrid (1,708 men). June 1808: Impressed into French service. Fought against the Spanish at Alcolea (6 June) and captured at Bailén (19 July). Most chose to serve in the Spanish Army.

Flags - *Suizo de Courten* and *de Preux* (1796-1808) had white field with red alternate flames, a large red cross and in the corners the Valais coat of arms.[128]

6° **Suizo de Preux**

Summerfield, 2013

Uniforms of the Swiss Infantry

It is unclear whether the Swiss infantry received their new M1805 uniform because the old M1796 uniform was shown in the 1805 and 1806 editions of *Reglamento de Uniformidaddel Ejército y la Marina en 1805*.

M1796

Summerfield, 2013

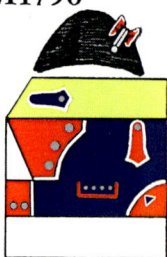

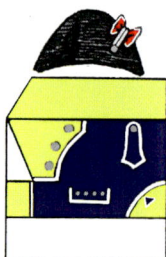

| 1º Suizo de Wimpffen | 2º Suizo de Reding Snr | 3º Suizo de Reding Jnr |

M1796

Summerfield, 2013

| 4º Suizo de Betschartd | 5º Suizo de Traxler | 6º Suizo de Prenx |

HEADWEAR: Black bicorn. From 1767, the Swiss had the honour to edge their large red cockades with white.

Grenadiers wore the tall black bearskin cap with long heavily embroidered triangular bag in regimental facing colour with tassel.

COAT: Blue coat with scarlet cuffs and lapels piped white except *4º Suizo de Betschartd* with yellow facings. The regiments were distinguisted by their collars and cuff designs. .

BUTTONS: White metal buttons except *5º Suizo de Traxler.*

DISTINCTIONS: Officers had epaulettes in button colour and scarlet sash.

LEGWEAR: White breeches with black gaiters and shoes.

Table 5: Old "M1796" Swiss Infantry uniform

	Cuffs and lapels	Collar	Turnback	Piping	Buttons
1º Suizo de Wimpffen	Scarlet	Yellow with blue buttonhole	Scarlet	White	White
2º Suizo de Reding Snr	Scarlet	Scarlet	Scarlet	White	White
3º Suizo de Reding Jnr	Scarlet	Yellow	Scarlet	White	White
4º Suizo de Betschartd	Yellow	Yellow	Yellow	White	White
5º Suizo de Traxler	Scarlet	Scarlet	White	White	Brass
6º Suizo de Courten/Preux	Scarlet	Blue	Scarlet	White	White

Clonard (1851) suggests that the Swiss Regiments received a new pattern uniform based upon the M1805 uniform by 1808 but this has not be established.

M1805

Summerfield, 2013

1º-5º Suizo   **6º Suizo de Preux**

HEADWEAR: As above.

COAT: Blue coat with scarlet piped white collar, lapels, cuffs and shoulder strap. Blue cuff flap. . *6º Suizo de Preux* had blue collar and red cuff flaps instead.

BUTTONS: White metal buttons.

DISTINCTIONS: Officers had epaulettes in button colour and scarlet sash.

LEGWEAR: White breeches with black gaiters and shoes.

Table 6: New "M1805" Swiss Infantry uniform was probably not issued

	Cuffs and Lapels	Collar	Turnbacks	Buttons
1º-5º Suizo	Scarlet	Red with blue buttonhole	Scarlet	White
6º Suizo de Preux	Scarlet	Blue	Scarlet	White

Catalonia Light Infantryman and Artilleryman
[Bradford, 1809]

Chapter 7
Cazadores (Light Infantry)

There were twelve light infantry regiments in the Spanish Army. The Royal Order of 26 August 1802 stipulated that each regiment would comprise a single battalion of six companies.

Battalion Command:

1 commander (*coronel* or *teniente coronel*), 1 *sargento mayor* (major), 1 *capitán ayudante,* (adjutant captain), 1 *teniente ayudante* (adjutant lieutenant), 1 *subteniente abanderado* (2nd lt standard-bearer), 1 *tambor mayor* (drum major), 1 *capellan* (chaplain), 1 *cirujano* (surgeon), 1 *maestro armero* (master armourer).

Company

1 *capitán* (captain), 1 *capitán segundo* (2nd captain), 2 *tenientes* (1st lt), 2 *subtenientes* (2nd lt), 1 *sargento primero* (1st sergeant), 5 *sargentos segundos* (2nd sergeants), 8 *cabos primeros* (corporals), 8 *cabos segundos* (lance corporals), 3 *tambores* (drummers), 105 *soldados* (soldiers).

In peacetime, each battalion had 39 officers and 780 men. This was raised to 1,200 men when fully mobilised with the addition of 70 soldiers per company. In 1808, many of these battalions were over strength and it was common practice for them to operate in half-battalions of three companies where they operated independently even in different armies.

La Romana's Light Infantry
Augsburger, 1807

Cazadores Flags

Each single battalion *Cazadores* Regiments had one *Coronela* and one *Sencilla* flag. Many of the new issue flags in 1796 were of the new combined *Coronela* and *Sencilla* design. On 26 August 1802, the flags were reduced to one *Coronela* flag.

Coronela of 1° Voluntarios de Aragon (Est. 1762)

1° Voluntarios de Aragón (Est. 1762)

Voluntarios de Aragón was created 19 February 1762. In 1793, it was renamed *1° Voluntarios de Aragón* upon the creation of a second regiment.

Campaign History: In May 1808, the Bn was in Madrid (1,305 men). In Saragossa with 1215 men in September 1808 and fought at Tudela (23 Nov). Then participated in the defence of Saragossa (19 Dec 1808-20 Feb 1809).

Flag - Carried the *Coronela* flag.

1º Bn de Voluntarios de Cataluña (Est. 1762)

Created on 19 February 1762. Under Major J. F. Viven, this large battalion was the finest light infantry available from Spain trained in French tactics and drill. Absorbed *Rgto Hoya de Málaga* (12 May 1812) on 1 July 1812. Absorbed *Tiradores de Cataluña* (Est. 7 Nov 1811) and on 2 March 1815.

Campaign History: In May 1808, it was part of the *División del Norte* in Denmark (1,164 men) In September 1808 it escaped with La Romana from Denmark. Later it was part 5th (La Romana) Division of Blake's Army of Galicia that fought at Valmaseda (5 Nov), at Espinosa (10-11 Nov), and reduced to 57 men on 16 Feb 1809. It was part of the Vanguard of MG de la Carrera at Alba de Tormes and defeated at Uclés (13 Jan 1809), part of defence of Saragossa (19 Dec 1808-20 Feb 1809). Part of the Lines of Torres Vedras (1810-11). Part of 3rd (Ballesteros) Division at Albuera (16 May 1811).

1º Bn de Voluntarios de Cataluña (Est. 1762)

Flag - Carried the *Coronela* flag with royal arms in the centre.

2º Bn de Voluntarios de Cataluña (Est. 1762)

Created on 19 February 1762 as the *2º Rgto de Voluntarios de Cataluña*. In 1792, renamed *2º Bn de Infantería Ligera de Cataluña*. In 1802, renamed *2º Bn de Voluntarios de Cataluña*.

Campaign History: Defence of Melilla (1774-75). Expedition to Algiers (1775). Siege of Gibraltar (1779). Expeditions to New Orleans, Pensacola and Santo Domingo (1780-82). In the Roussillon Campaign (1793-95), part of the combats of Azcárate, Bristles and Urquía. Revolution in Bilbao (1804). In 1805, detachments acted as Marines on Spanish ships at Trafalgar (21 Oct) and expedition to Martinique. In May 1808, a Bn was in La Coruña (685 men) Part of the Army of Galicia and fought at Medina de Rioseco (14 July), Zornoza (30 Oct) and Gamonal (10 Nov). In 1809, fought at Medellín (29 Mar), Talavera (27 July), Medina del Campo and Alba de Tormes. In 1811, present at Torres-Vedras, Saint Engracia, Albuera, siege of Cádiz, reconquest of Pancorbo, place of Pamplona, combats of San Marcial and los Angeles.

Flag - Carried the *Coronela* flag.

Voluntarios de Gerona (Est. 1792)

The Regulation of 3 June 1792 ordered the formation of *Rgto de Voluntarios de Gerona* by D. Francisco Martí. It was not formed until 5 November 1792. Absorbed *Cazadores del Rey* (1 July 1809) on 2 March 1815.

Campaign History: Roussillon Campaign (1793-95) and war with Portugal (1801). In May 1808, a half Bn was in Portugal and the other half Bn in San Roque (1,149 men) Later part of the Army of Galicia and fought at Zornoza (30 Oct). In the Americas (1816-24).

Flag - Carried the *Coronela* flag with royal arms in the centre.

Voluntarios de Tarragona (Est. 1792)

Created by the Regulation of 3 June 1792. Raised by Coronel Don Vicente María Cañas Portocarrero Trelles y Silva Marqués de Castrillo y de Vallecerrato in Barcelona as *Rgto de Voluntarios de Infantería Ligera de Tarragona* on 31 August 1792.

Campaign History: Fought in the Roussillon Campaign (1793-94). In 1801 it moved to Merida and in 1802 to Campo de Gibraltar where its organisation was modified. In May 1808, a half Bn Vicente and a half Bn Pamplona (1,142 men). Joined the Army of Catalonia. Fought at the defence of Gerona, Saragossa, Palamós, San Feliu and La Bisbal.

2° Voluntarios de Aragón (Est. 1793)

Formed by Royal Order on 30 April 1793.

Campaign History: In May 1808, the Bn was in Mallorca (1,225 men). Joined the Army of Aragon (1275 men) in July 1808. Participated in the defence of Saragossa (19 Dec 1808-20 Feb 1809). On 4 January 1809, it was reorganised into 2 Bns of 6 coys.

Flag - Carried the *Coronela* flag.

1° Voluntarios de Barcelona (Est. 1793)

Created by Royal Order on 27 March 1793. Absorbed *Vol. Literarios de Santiago* (Est. 11 June 1808) on 2 March 1815.

Campaign History: In May 1808 it was part of the *División del Norte* in Denmark (1,266 men). Returned to Spain in September 1808 and joined the Army of Catalonia. In 1809, it fought at Valmaseda (5 Nov), Espinosa (10-11 Nov) with 900 men. In 1811, it was destroyed at Río Gévora (19 Feb).

Flag - Carried the "new" combined *Coronela* and *Sencilla* flag design of the Cross of Burgundy and royal arms in the centre.

2° Voluntarios de Barcelona (Est. 1793)

Created by Royal Order on 27 March 1793.

Campaign History

In May 1808, a Bn was in Menorca (1,300 men). Joined the Army of Catalonia and fought at the defence of Rosas (7 Nov-5 Dec 1808) and the defence of Gerona (6 June-10 Dec 1809).

Flag - Carried the *Sencilla* flag.

2° Voluntarios de
Barcelona (Est. 1792)

Voluntarios de Valencia (Est. 1794)

Voluntarios de Valencia was created on 1 May 1794.

Campaign History

In May 1808, a half Bn Portugal and the other half Bn in Tarifa (1,242 men) Later joined the Army of Catalonia.

Flag - Carried the *Coronela* flag with royal arms in the centre.

Cazadores Voluntarios de Barbastro (Est. 1794)

Cazadores de Montaña de la Ciudad de Barbastro was created on 20 April 1793 by Colonel D. Diego de Alcega. In 1794, renamed *Rgto de Cazadores Voluntarios de Barbastro*. In mid 1808, two units were formed around cadres from unit.

- *Tercio de Barbastro,* Renamed *Torrero* (13 Nov 1808).
- *Bn de la Reunión Osera* was formed from 300 men from Osera, Pina de Ebro, Velilla and Gelsa by D. António Guerrero. Changed name to *Bn de Tiradores de Doyle*[129] and commanded by D. Miguel Eraso. In 1811 (some authors state it as 1814), this was renamed *Rgto de Infantería Cazadores de Barbastro.*

Cazadores Voluntarios de Barbastro
(Est. 1794)

On 2 March 1815, the regiment was reformed from *Vol. Numantinos* (Est. 2 June 1808).

Campaign History: 1794-95: Pyrenees campaign against France. 1801: war with Portugal. 1802: reduced to a Bn with the name of *Bn de Infantería Ligera Cazadores de*

---

[129] In the honour of British General Sir William Doyle.

Barbastro. 1804-06: Blockade of Gibraltar. 1807: Divided into two parts, one in Portugal and the other one in Campo de Gibraltar. May 1808: a half Bn was in San Roque and a half Bn in Portugal (1,061 men). One half Bn in the Army of Galicia fought at Medina de Rioseco (14 July). The other half Bn in the Army of Andalusia fought at Bailén (19 July). Two units were formed around cadres.

- *Tercio de Barbastro* (1,022) fought at Zornoza (30 Oct). Almost destroyed at Uclés (13 Jan 1809) and reduced to 63 men by 16 Feb.
- *Rgto de Infantería Cazadores de Barbastro* fought at Albuera, Espinosa, Tamames, Villafranca, Lugo and siege of Saragossa. In 1815 it was renamed *Rgto Segundo de Cazadores de Barbastro* when it embarked for Venezuela.

In 1815, the reformed regiment served in Venezuela until 1821.

Flag - Carried the *Coronela* flag with royal arms in the centre. Depicted above is the *Sencilla* that was deposited in 1802 in a church in Pueyo and was reused by the new battalion of volunteers.

Campo Maior (Est. 1802)

Formed on 26 August 1802 as *Bn Ligero de Campo Maior* commanded by D. Cayetano Iriarte. Absorbed *Vol. de Villanueva de los Infantes* (Est. 2 June 1808) on 27 December 1808.

Campaign History: 1805: As Marines at Cape Finisterre (22 July) and Trafalgar (21 Oct). 1807: Occupation of Setúbal, Portugal. May 1808: half Bn in Portugal and half at San Roque (1,153) 1809: Almost destroyed at Uclés (13 Jan). Fought at Mesa de Ibor (17 Mar) and Medellín (29 Mar). 1815: *Rgto de Infantería Ligera La Albuera*. Suppressed by Royal Decree of 1 June 1818.

Flag - Carried the *Coronela* flag with royal arms in the centre.

Voluntarios de Navarra (Est. 1802)

Formed on 26 August 1802 as *Bn de Infantería Ligera de Voluntarios de Navarra*. In 1811, it was renamed the *Bn de Infantería Ligera Voluntarios de Navarra*. In 1812, renamed to *Voluntarios de Navarra Ligero*. Suppressed by Royal Decree of 1 June 1818.

Campaign History: 1806: Expedition to Portugal and defence of the Ferrol. May 1808: half Bn in Portugal and half Bn at Ferrol (963). Joined the Army of Galicia. Fought at Medina de Rioseco (14 July) and Zornoza (30 Oct).

Flag - Carried the *Coronela* flag with royal arms in the centre.

M1800 *Cazadores* Uniform

The original *Cazadores* uniform was a black bicorn and green coat with red cuffs and lapels, white waistcoat and knee length gaiters. This changed to a blue coat in emulation of the French *Légère*. In 1800, the uniform had the appearance of Republican French Infantry except for the brown leather knee length gaiters.

HEADWEAR: Black bicorn.

COAT: Blue coat with red facings.

WAISTCOAT: White waistcoat edged red.

GREATCOAT: Green greatcoat.

LEGWEAR: White breeches, brown leather knee length gaiters and black or brown leather shoes.

EQUIPMENT: White belts and black leather ventral cartridge box.

Voluntarios
de Barbastro, 1800

M1802 Cazadores Officer's headwear [Suhr]

M1802 *Cazadores* Uniform

In 1802, a dashing Hussar inspired uniform was authorised.

HEADWEAR: Leather helmet with black fur crest and brass furniture similar to the British Tarleton. The national cockade was on the left side under the green plume. The oval brass plate bore the Spanish coat of arms.

M1802 Cacadores helmets [Suhr]

The forage cap similar to the French *bonnet-de-police*. Officers wore either bicorns or the Tarleton Helmets.

M1802 Cacadores bonnet-de-police
By Christoph Suhr

Vaughan Funnell

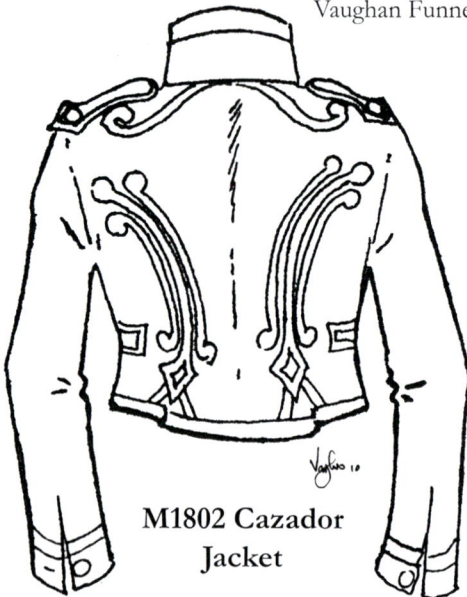

TUNIC: Green laced dolman style jacket with red collar and cuffs, yellow lace and a red sash.

BUTTONS: Brass.

CLOAK: A short brown cloak worn over the left shoulder was often worn due to the lack of issue of greatcoats.

LEGWEAR: Green breeches. Often native sandals and leggings were worn in place of heavy shoes and gaiters.

M1802 Cazador Jacket

M1802 Cazador Uniforms

Cazador

Officer

Officer in surtout

Musician

EQUIPMENT: White leather belts, brown or black leather belly cartridge box and infantry short sword.

1º Bn de Voluntarios
de Cataluña

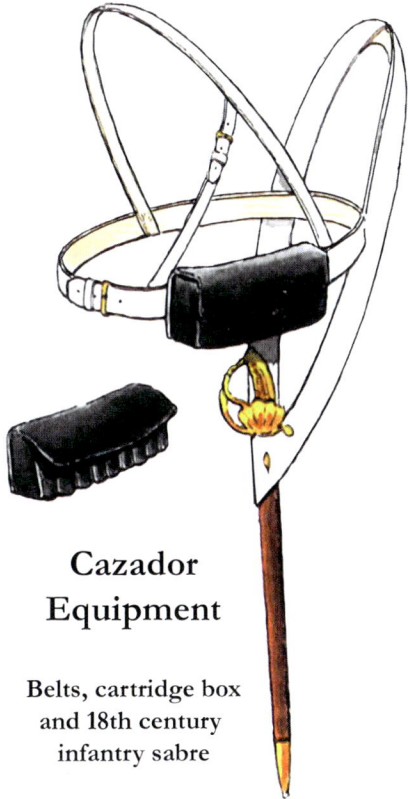

Cazador Equipment

Belts, cartridge box and 18th century infantry sabre

Cazadores in M1802 Uniform
By Bueno

Parade Dress

Undress

Officer

Plate 15: *1° Cazadores de Cataluña*
By Christoph Suhr

The three figures depicted wear the M1802 light cavalry style dolman with the appropriate lace on the back. Note the shades of green shown in the plates. In reality green was a notoriously difficult colour to dye. In this case of emerald green, the yellow component tended to fade quickly. The two officers on the left wear the form of town dress of dolmans casually undone as was the Spanish custom. The lieutenant (left) has a green fluffy plume and the officer (centre) has his plume encased in a waterproof cover. The soldier on the right carries the *escopeta* (a short light infantry musket from Catalonia), and wears *alpargatas* sandals, the preferred form of light footwear favoured by the Spanish.

Plate 16: *Cazadores de Barcelona* and *de Cataluña*
By Christoph Suhr

(1): The regimental barber of the *1° Cazadores de Barcelona* carries his shaving mug with lid and a brass bowl for holding hot water to shave his clients. It was a useful way to supplement his low pay as a soldier.

(2): The officer's servant carries his master's lunch in a leather lattice bag. Status was important to Spanish officers and it was a matter of personal honour to have a servant. He wears the undress red jacket with a striped blue and red shirt adorned with brass buttons. His attire is complete with a jaunty top pie hat festooned with a plume.

(3): The *Cazador de Barcelona* is comfortably attired for the march ahead, with his slung brown cloak and civilian breeches. Note the "VB" badge plate barely visible on his *bonnet-de-police*.

(4): His colleague from the *1° Cazadores de Cataluña* is dressed in a similar fashion, adopting an even more relaxed stance, down to the inordinately long *bonnet-de-police*.

(5): The *Cazador* on the far right is in full dress. His green plumed helmet is visible above the standard brown cloak.

Plate 17: *Cazador* with his wife and two children
By Christoph Suhr

This plate shows a soldier of the *1° Cazadores de Cataluña* crouched around a fire with his family enjoying a meal, dressed collectively against the cold. The only vestiges of regulation M1802 uniform visible are the *bonnet-de-police* the main body being in emerald green and scarlet edged in yellow, the ubiquitous brown cloak covering the uniform. His son seems to be wearing a spare cap of his father's. He was originally part of the Etruria Expeditionary Force that left Spain in 1806 so did not receive the new M1805 uniform until January 1808 just before they left Hamburg for Denmark.

Plate 18: *1º Cazadores de Barcelona* in civilian clothes

By Christoph Suhr

Often the Spanish wore civilian clothes when not on parade. These five stalwart gentlemen of the *1º Cazadores de Barcelona* are suitably attired in their civilian clothes, a common practise among La Romana's troops to save wear and tear on their expensive and precious uniforms. The uniforms themselves were of a high quality, much thicker than today, of a hard wearing worsted wool. A uniform coat for example was to last for a minimum of two and a half years, before being replaced. Note the assortment of head attire. Striped clothing of blue and white was popular and it was not uncommon to wear ticken trousers made from mattress covers as in Republican France just over the border.

Plate 19: Soldier of the *1° Cazadores de Cataluña* with his wife on a mule

By Christoph Suhr

Note the habit of binding both mule and horse tails partly for show and no doubt for cleanliness. Of interest is the M1802 *bonnet-de-police* festooned with the emblem of the *Cataluña* light infantry, being a hand sewn badge in the form of a shield quartered with a red cross on a white background top left and right, the other two corners comprising equal red and yellow stripes in a green leaf garland. He carries his civilian clothes in the popular chequered cloth bag.

~ 139 ~

Plate 20: A *Cazador* with his family on the march
By Christoph Suhr

Similar in composition to the previous plate, the *Cazador de Barcelona* has what appears to be the favourite form of undress uniform worn on the march, no doubt the light sandals add to this comfortable get up. His *Barcelona* light infantry regimental brass badge (a shield badge enclosed in a wreath) is clearly visible. Again the favourite brown cloak is much in evidence. His wife is riding side saddle on the donkey an early form of riding rig.

Plate 21: *Cazador de Barcelona* **with his family**
By Christoph Suhr

This pleasing portrait of domestic harmony shows the strong bonds present in La Romana Division as this force was accompanied by a huge baggage train, wives and children, and all the impedimenta they carried including livestock. In this case the *Cazador de Barcelona* is wearing a civilian style brown greatcoat and top hat carries his guitar and his musket is slung over his shoulder. His wife and child are astride the donkey which carries to all intents and purposes his worldly possessions including his precious uniform, his sabre briquette and umbrella being clearly visible jutting out of the bundle.

Plate 22: Officer's servant of the *1° Cazadores de Cataluña*
By Christoph Suhr

This is an interesting character of a slightly more motley appearance then his compatriots with his double buttoned waistcoat under his regimental jacket. The hooded cloak looks to be privately purchased. Astride his master's mule he looks the picture of relaxation smoking the new and fashionable *cigarrillos*. Intensive mule farming had taken over in Spain from horse breeding for practical reasons due to the extreme temperatures and poor roads, not to mention a chronic lack of funds.

Plate 23: Officers of the *1° Cazadores de Barcelona* [Suhr].

The trio of Officers depicted in this plate are all effectively in variations of the regimental full dress. Subtle differences tell them apart from the variety of gold Hungarian lace on their tight pantaloons. The lieutenant on the right is wearing a long tailed *surtout*. The captain in the centre has a gilded light cavalry sabre while his two companions sport gilded black leather infantry sabres. Note the variance in plume sizes.

Plate 24: Captain of *1° Cazadores de Barcelona* riding a mule

By Christoph Suhr

The Captain of the *Barcelona* light infantry astride the diminutive mule is characterised by his unadorned "fore and aft" bicorn apart from gold bullion tassels at the tip. Spanish Army Officers were allowed a fair amount of latitude in manner of dress. The only items being *de rigueur* were badges of rank and a suitable sabre. In this case a gilded straight bladed epee is worn in lieu of the normal regimental variety of sabre. Short blue-grey breeches are unusual, the plain leather saddle less so.

Bandsmen

Bandsmen had the same style uniform but their jackets were blue with white buttons and braid.

Plate 25: Lady and Musician *1° Cazadores de Cataluña*
By Christoph Suhr

The lady sutleress accompanies a member of the Catalonian Band of the *Cataluña* light infantry regiment. The large sized drum was probably constructed of a lighter brass shell and hide to enable the musician to carry it on his back! He is effectively wearing full national costume carrying in addition to a fan and the ever present umbrella.

Plate 26: Soldiers and Musician of *1º Cazadores de Cataluña*
By Christoph Suhr

This plate comprises a collection of soldiers and musicians in M1802 uniform. Known for their exotic costumes this "Jingling Johnny" is no exception, in his blue jacket favoured by musicians of this regiment with crimson braid resembling a British light dragoon, sporting a Tarleton helmet. The scarlet stable jacket worn by two of the soldiers appears to be their *uniforme de marcha*. Adorned with two sets of brass buttons this was a very functional item of attire. Note the variety of trousers worn. Bueno (1990) also gives buff, sky-blue and white striped trousers for this unit. The greatcoat worn by the musician with his back to us is likely to have been of local German manufacture rather than the usual brown cloak.

New M1805 *Cazadores* Uniform

1º Voluntarios de Aragón

Reglamento de Uniformidad del Ejército y la Marina en 1805

In 1806, a new uniform was authorised of a similar cut to the line infantry but in dark blue. The introduction of this uniform took over two years to reach the regiments.

HEADWEAR: Bicorn with red cockade.

TUNIC: Dark blue coat with collar, cuffs, turnbacks and trim in regimental colour. Dark blue waistcoat.

GREATCOAT: Brown greatcoat.

LEGWEAR: White breeches with black gaiters. Black shoes.

EQUIPMENT: The cartridge belt was carried on the white shoulder belt rather than the regulation belly box. Black tipped brass bayonet and sword scabbard.

1º Voluntarios de Cataluña

Voluntarios de Valencia

Table 7: M1805 *Cazadores* uniform details[130]

Light Infantry	Collar	Cuffs & Cuff flaps	Turnbacks	Lapels	Pocket Piping	Buttons
1° de Aragón	Red piped white	Red piped white	Red	Red piped white	Red	White metal
1° de Cataluña	Yellow	Yellow piped white	Yellow	Yellow piped white	Yellow	Brass
2° de Cataluña	Dark blue piped white	Yellow cuffs piped white & yellow cuff flap	Yellow	Yellow	Yellow	Brass
Tarragona	Yellow	Yellow	Yellow	Dark Blue piped yellow	Yellow	Brass
Gerona	Yellow	Yellow	Yellow	Yellow piped white	Yellow	White metal
2° de Aragón	Dark. blue piped white	Red piped white	Red piped white	Red piped white	Red	White metal
1° de Barcelona	Yellow	Yellow	Yellow	Dark blue piped white	Yellow	White metal
2° de Barcelona	Dark blue piped white	Yellow	Yellow	Yellow	Yellow	White metal
Barbastro	Red piped white	Red piped white	Red piped white	Dark blue piped white	White	White metal
Vol. de Valencia	Crimson piped white	Crimson piped white	Crimson piped white	Crimson piped white	White	White metal
Campo Maior	Dark blue piped white	Crimson piped white	Crimson piped white	Crimson piped white	White	White metal
Vol. de Navarra	Crimson piped white	Crimson piped white	Crimson piped white	Dark blue piped white	White	White metal

[130] Bueno (1982) pp72-73

Summerfield, 2013

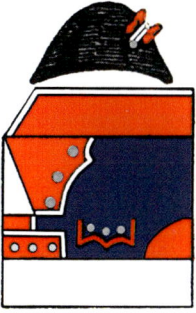

1º de Aragón
(1762)

1º de Cataluña
(1762)

2º de Cataluña
(1762)

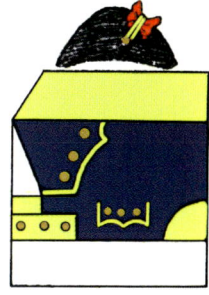

Tarragona
(1792)

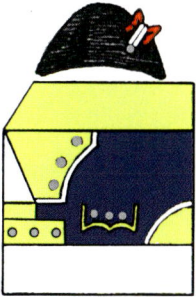

Gerona
(1792)

2º de Aragón
(1793)

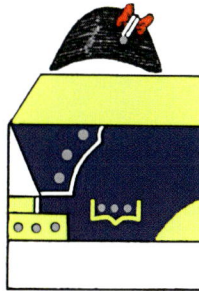

1º de Barcelona
(1793)

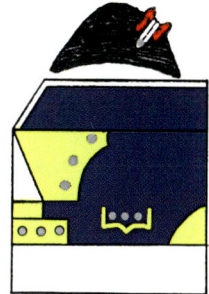

2º de Barcelona
(1793)

Barbastro
(1794)

Vol. de Valencia
(1794)

Campo Maior
(1802)

Vol. de Navarra
(1802)

Cazadores M1805 uniform

1º Voluntarios de Aragón

1º Voluntarios de Cataluña

2º Voluntarios de Cataluña

Voluntarios de Gerona

Cazadores M1805 uniform
Reglamento de Uniformidad del Ejército y la Marina en 1806

Voluntarios de Tarragona

2º Voluntarios de Aragón

1º Voluntarios de Barcelona

2º Voluntarios de Barcelona

Cazadores M1805 uniform

Reglamento de Uniformidad del Ejército y la Marina en 1806

Cazadores de Barbastro

Voluntarios de Valencia

Voluntarios de Campo Mayor

Voluntarios de Navarra

Cazadores M1805 uniform

Reglamento de Uniformidad del Ejército y la Marina en 1806

New M1805 Uniform for La Romana's *Cazadores*

The *Cazadores de Cataluña* and *Cazadores de Barcelona* received the M1805 uniform just before departing Hamburg for Denmark in January 1808. This was made in Paris so it shows some differences from the Spanish 1805 regulations. This included a French light infantry shakos with the brass accoutrements from their old helmets instead of regulation bicorns.

HEADWEAR: Instead of the in January 1808, the two *Cazadores* battalions received French manufactured shakos with a shako plate and cords in the button colour. The green plume surmounting the red cockade from their bicorns was mounted on the left hand side of the shako.[131]

M1805 Light Infantry Shako [Suhr]

TUNIC: Dark blue coat with collar, cuffs, turnbacks and trim in regimental colour. Dark blue waistcoat.

GREATCOAT: Brown greatcoat.

LEGWEAR: White breeches with black gaiters. Black shoes.

EQUIPMENT: The cartridge belt on the white shoulder belt rather than the regulation belly box. Black tipped brass bayonet and sword scabbard.

1° Cazadores de Barcelona in new uniform, c1808

---

[131] The 1st Barcelona *Cazadores* had a white metal oval shako plate inscribed with "I. DE BARCELONA" and white cords. The 1st *Cazadores de Cataluña* had a diamond brass plate inscribed with "I. DE CATALUÑA" and yellow shako cords.

M1805 uniforms made in Paris

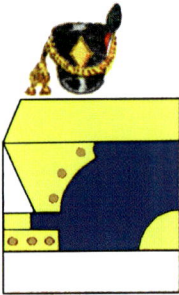
Cazador

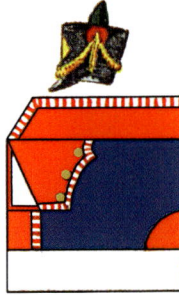
Drummer

Musician

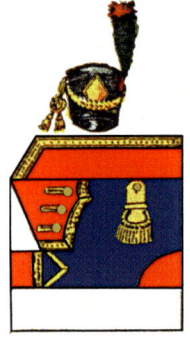
Drum Major

1° Cazadores de Cataluña
unique to La Romana's Division in Denmark [Summerfield, 2013]

Plate 27: Drum-major of the *1° Cazadores de Cataluña* and musicians of *Regimiento de la Princesa*
By Christoph Suhr

Drum-major of the *1° Cazadores de Cataluña* on the right shows the height of Spanish elegance in his new M1805 long tailed dark blue jacket faced scarlet with an abundance of gold bullion on his splendid hand embroidered sash and oversized green plume. His baton is topped in sterling silver.

His two companions decked out in scarlet are two musicians from the *Regimiento de la Princesa*. They are also in the new M1805 red uniform issued just prior to their embarkation to Denmark. The French influence is clearly apparent with the oversized colpaks, falling flame and thin high white egret plumes.

The child playing the flute wears a black colpak with red Busby bag edged white and white plume. The red dolman has dark blue facings, white lace and buttons. He wears white trousers and Hessian boots. The musician playing the cymbals wears a black colpak with red Busby bag edged white and white plume. The red dolman has dark blue facings, white lace and buttons.

Plate 28: Musicians and soldier of the *1º Cazadores de Cataluña* in their new uniform

By Christoph Suhr

This plate shows the dawn of a new era for the uniforms of the Spanish Infantry. As a relatively wealthy regiment they commissioned in Hamburg the French inspired M1805 uniform with short tailed *surtouts* and bell topped shako. The soldier's facings were dull yellow. Note the musicians' facing colour of scarlet edged yellow a happy combination of colours, topped with a resplendent green plume. The regiment seems only to have been partially issued the new uniform as the older M1802 was still in use. The shako plate reads "1 DE CATALUÑA" stamped into the brass that later became a common distinction with Spanish regimental plates.

Chapter 8
Militia

Philip V gave the first effective organisation to the 33 *Milicia Provincial* (Provincial Militia) Regiments on 31 January 1734. When the war began in 1808, there were 42 Provincial Militia Regiments (43 Bns) in Spain and 114 of Urban Militia battalions.

Milicia Provincial (Provincial Militia)

New regulations for the militia were authorised in 19 June 1802. In 1804, the provincial militia was mobilised because of the threat of British landing parties and were considered at a similar level of efficiency as the line infantry.[132] There were 42 Provincial Militia Regiments. All had a single battalion, except the Mallorca militia with two battalions. The organisation was changed again on 27 October 1806. Each battalion had four fusilier companies and one grenadier company.

> **Staff**: 1 *coronel*, 1 *sargento mayor* (major), 1 *ayudante*, 1 *tambor mayor* (drum-major), 1 *capellan*, 1 *maestro armero* (master armourer), 1 *asesor*, 1 *escribano*.
>
> **Fusilier company**: 1 *capitán*, 2 *tenientes*, 2 subtenientes, 1 *sargento primero*, 4 *sargentos segundos*, 3 *tambores*, 8 *cabos primeros*, 8 *cabos segundos*, 134 *fusileros*.

M1802 Provincial Militia Uniform

A blue or brown coat with red facings introduced in 1802.

HEADWEAR: Black bicorn with red cockade and plume.

COAT: Deep sky blue coat with red facings edged white. The colour varied according to the quality of the cloth and the amount of dye. Many of the coats were already 6 years old so would have faded considerably in the sun. The M1802 provisional was brown with red facings edged white.

WAISTCOAT: White waistcoat.

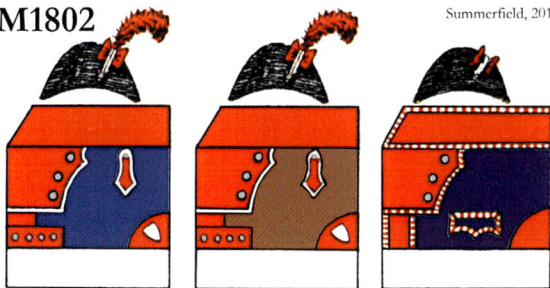

M1802

Summerfield, 2013

Fusilier · Provincial · Drummer

Provincial Militia

DISTINCTIONS: Officers had epaulettes in button colour. Drummer wore a dark blue coat with red and white lace.

LEGWEAR: White breeches with black gaiters. Breeches were often replaced by long brown or checked trousers. Black shoes.

---

[132] Sanudo (1999) p152

M1805 Provincial Militia Uniform

A new M1805 white uniform was introduced in 1805 but did not replace most of the older uniforms. The *inspector general de milicias*, Pedro Mendiueta[133], on 16 May 1808 reported that most regiments were wearing the M1802 brown uniform (17 Bns), M1802 blue (2 Bns), without uniforms (2 Bns), M1805 white (1 Bns) and the remaining 21 battalions had uniforms of unknown origin (pp279-280).[134]

Fusilier and Officer of the Provincial Militia, c1806

Reglamento de Uniformidad del Ejercito y la Marina en 1805

M1805

Fusilier · Officer

Provincial Militia uniform

HEADWEAR: Black bicorn with large red cockade.

COAT: White coat and turnbacks. White waistcoat.

DISTINCTIONS: Officers had epaulettes in button colour. Drummer wore a dark blue coat with red and white lace.

LEGWEAR: White breeches with black gaiters. Breeches were often replaced by long brown or checked trousers. Black shoes.

---

[133] Pedro Mendiueta (1736-1825) was *inspector general de milicias* and a Supreme Council of War member.
[134] Mendinueta (16 May 1808) *Noticia de las Provincias y Destinos que tienen en ellas los 8 Batallones de las 4 Divisiones de Granaderos y los 42 Regimientos de Milicias…..*, Madrid.

Provincial Militia Uniforms in May 1808

Table 8: *Milicia Provincial* (Provincial Militia) uniforms
[Pedro Mendinueta (16 May 1808), Madrid]

Milicia Provincial	Position May 1808	Position May 1808
Alcazar	Sanlúcar de Barrameda, Andalusia	M1802 brown
Avila	Alicante, Murcia	M1802 brown
Burgos	Jerez de la Frontera, Andalusia	M1802 brown
Buxalance	Sanlúcar de Barrameda, Andalusia	M1802 brown
Ciudad Rodrigo	Isla de León, Andalusia	M1802 brown
Ciudad Real	Puerto de St Maria, Andalusia	Without uniforms
Cuenca	Tarifa, Andalusia	M1802 brown
Ecija	Cádiz, Andalusia	M1802 brown
Granada	Isla de León, Andalusia	M1802 brown
Jaén	Algeciras, Andalusia	M1802 brown
Laredo	Santander, Asturias	M1802 blue
Lorca	Algeciras, Andalusia	M1802 brown
Mondonedo	Ferrol, Galicia	M1802 brown
Murcia	Cartagena, Murcia	Useless uniforms
Oviedo	Gifon, Asturias	M1802 blue
Ronda	Cádiz, Andalusia	M1802 brown
Sevilla	Jerez de la Frontera, Andalusia	M1802 brown
Siguenza	Quartel de Buenabina, Andalusia	M1805 white
Soria	Valencia, Murcia	M1802 brown
Toro	Isla de León, Andalusia	M1802 brown
Trujillo	Puerto de St Maria, Andalusia	M1802 brown
Tuy	Ferrol, Galicia	M1802 brown

Table 9: Unknown *Rgto de Milicia Provincial* (Provincial Militia) uniforms
[Pedro Mendinueta (16 May 1808), Madrid]

Milicia Provincial	Position May 1808	*Milicia Provincial*	Position May 1808
Badajóz	Ayamonte, Andalusia	Malaga	Los Barrios, Galicia
Betanzos	Coruña, Galicia	Monterrey	Ferrol, Galicia
Chinchilla	Estepona, Andalusia	Orense	Vigo, Andalusia
Compostella	Coruña, Galicia	Plasencia	Isla de León, Galicia
Córdoba	Cádiz, Andalusia	Pontevedra	Ferrol, Galicia
Guadix	San Roque, Andalusia	Salamanca	Momefaxo, Galicia
Jerez	Cádiz, Galicia	Santiago	Ferrol, Galicia
León	Ares, Andalusia	Segovia	Coruña, Andalusia
Logroño	Isla de León, Galicia	Toledo	Cádiz, Galicia
Lugo	Ferrol, Andalusia	Valladolid	Ares, Andalusia

Plate 29: *Rgto de Guadalajara and Milicia Provincial*
By Christoph Suhr

This is from Suhr (1808) and is one of the few representations of figures that are repeated in Suhr (1818). It has the addition of a lush background and the figures being drawn in greater detail indicating that this was a painting rather than a sketch from life. The figure second from the right is unusually in his white 1805 full dress uniform that is rarely seen in both series. An even rarer depiction is a side view of the Spanish smoothbore M1801 brass bound musket that was 0.69-inch calibre, a sturdy weapon by all accounts. Drafts from the Militia Provincial were attached to the artillery. The militia (left) swathed in a brown cloak wears M1802 brown coat with red facings piped white. The other militiaman (right) wears a M1802 blue coat with red facings with red facings.

Milicias Provinciales Flags

In 1734, each regiment had three white taffeta flags. The *Coronela* had the royal coat of arms in the centre. The other two had a shield of the provinces with ducal crowns at the ends of the red Cross of Burgundy and their name over the breadth of the flag at the top. Flagstaffs were eleven *pies* high. This was in practice almost identical to the M1728 infantry flag.[135]

M1802

On 27 March 1754, the King approved a contract with Pablo Oliver and Leopoldo Ferrara for the construction of the new *Sencillas* flags for the 33 Militia Regiments. These were similar to the M1748 infantry flag but again with ducal crowns on the shields rather than royal ones. However, the *Coronelas* were not replaced.[136]

In 1766, the 42 regiments each had one *Coronela* and one *Sencilla*. These were identical to the M1762 infantry flags with the shields in the corners with ducal crown. On 14 January 1769, the General Inspector of Militias instructed that their old flags of 1736 were to be deposited in churches.[137] Some Militia Regiments participated in the War of the First Coalition against the French and *de Tuy* received a battle honour for the retreat of Irún (1 Aug 1794). In 1802, as with the Infantry, the flags were reduced to just the *Coronela* and the *Sencilla* were withdrawn from service. Thus, during the Peninsular War they carried only the *Coronela*.[138] Some of the Provincial Militia Regiments still using ancient M1754 flags received during the reign of Fernando VI (r1746-59). These included *Milicias Provinciales de Oviedo* and *de Santiago*.

Provincial Militiaman
By Vaughan Funnell

The following descriptions were derived from Sorando Muzás (2008):[139]

Alcázar de San Juan: Mounted armed gentleman and a castle on top of a mount.

Avila. Embroidered blue castle with king on his battlements in a white field and surrounded by the motto AVILA DEL REY.

Badajóz: Red lion rampant supported in column with PLUS ULTRA, on white field.

---

[135] Sorando Muzás (2000) p73
[136] Sorando Muzás (2000) pp73-75
[137] Sorando Muzás (2000) pp75-76
[138] Sorando Muzás (2000) 76
[139] Sorando Muzás (2008) "Banderas de las Tropas españolas durante la Guerra de la Independencia" in *La Guerra de la Independencia (1808 – 1814), el pueblo español, su ejército y sus aliados frente a la ocupación napoleónica*, M. Defensa, pp. 331- 333

1809

Cuidad Rodrigo Militiaman
After Bueno

Betanzos: Bridge of three arches, with a tower on his centre on a blue field and with three yellow circles to each side.

Bujalance: Shield with yellow castle surrounded by a red border with seven yellow castles.

Burgos: Bust of a King with a red cloak and five yellow towers making a detour to his low half on white field.

Chinchilla: White castle with open drawbridge, two black eagles crowned on the tower and two deer.

Ciudad Real: Seated king under a canopy surmounted by a royal crown, surrounded with walled city and in a sky blue field.

Ciudad Rodrigo: Three white columns in blue field surrounded by the motto VERNACULA MIROBRIGENSI LEGIO.

Compostela: Tomb and star in a blue field.

Córdoba: Red lion rampant red on a white field surrounded with alternate border of yellow castles in red and from red lion on a white field.

Cuenca: Chalice with a star of eight tops on a red field.

Ecija: The radiant sun in a red field surrounded by the motto CIVITAS SOLIS VOCABITUR UNA.

Granada: Crowned natural pomegranate, between the letters F and Y also crowned on a white field.

Guadix: Shield divided into two parts: 1st yellow yoke and 2nd bundle of arrows on a white field.

Jaén: The coat of arms of the Ponce de León family consisting of two halves. The 1st with red lion rampant, and 2nd yellow with three red bars. These were surrounded by white border with seven red escutcheons with white central stripe.

Jerez: Blue and white alternate borders, with alternate border of Castile and León.

Laredo: Sky blue with a tower finished surmounted by three red flags and a script of the same colour but with white half moon, and to his feet the sea with three small vessels and a chain that separates them.

León: Red lion rampant on a white field.

Logroño: A bridge with three arcades and three towers, on a river and with blue border loaded with three yellow *fleur-de-lis*.

Lorca: Red with a castle between a sword and a key and with a king with sword and sceptre on the battlements. Around white border with motto LORCA SOLUM GRATUM CASTRUM SUPER ASTRA LOCATUM ENSIS MNIAS PRAVIS REGNI TUTISIMA CLAVIS.

Lugo: A tower on two reclining lions, and with a chalice on her, supported by two angels and with a radiant host, quite in white field.

Málaga: Walled city and the monogram MT.

Mondoñedo: Chalice with host surrounded with six yellow crosses and with the initials MO in a white field.

Monterrey: A tower in a white field with a lion rampant armed with sword on his battlements.

Murcia: Heart crowned in his centre with a lion and a *fleur-de-lis* and surrounded with seven open crowns, in celestial field, and around it borders alternates of yellow castles in red and red lion on a white field.

Orense: Lion with sabre in red field.

Oviedo: Golden cross supported by two angels in a celestial field.

Plasencia: A tower between a chestnut-tree and a pine in a white field.

Pontevedra: Bridge on a river with a cross in the centre and a tower at each end.

1809

Seville Miltiaman
After Bueno

Ronda: Arrows bundle, between two columns with the words "Plus Ultra," and under yellow yoke, quite in red field.

Salamanca: A bridge of three arcades, with a bull and a holm oak on a white field.

Santiago: Chalice with host on a white field.

Segovia. The aqueduct of Segovia with a head on it in a white or celestial field.

Seville: Possibly the anagram NO & DO on a white field, or San Fernando with world and sword in his hands.

Sigüenza: Formed by two halves: 1st a black eagle, and 2nd a castle on a red field.

Soria: Tower with a king on his battlements on a red field surrounded by the motto SORIA PURA CABEZA DE EXTREMADURA.

Spanish Insurgents, 1808
Old man on right wears a M1802
Militia Provincial jacket.

Toledo. Double-headed eagle under royal crown armed with the royal weapons and between two seated kings.

Toro: Shield divided into two halves: 1st black bull on a white field and 2nd red lion on a white field.

Trujillo: Fortified gate on a white field, and with Virgin and Child on the battlements.

Tuy: Rising moon with a face and three stars of six white tops, in a celestial field. To the feet of the royal shield it was showing embroidered that of distinction for the retreat of Irún (25 July 1794).

Valladolid. Six red wavy shreds on a yellow field and red border with eight yellow castles.

Granaderos Provinciales (Provincial Grenadiers)

**Table 10: *División de Granaderos Provinciales*
(Provincial Grenadier) uniforms**
[Pedro Mendinueta (16 May 1808), Madrid]

División de Granaderos Provinciales	May 1808	Uniform
I-II/ *de Castilla la Vieja*	Lisboa, Portugal	M1805 white
I-II/ *de Castilla la Nuevo*	Campo de Gibraltar, Andalusia	M1790 blue
I/ *de Andalucía*	Grana, Galicia	Useless uniforms
II/ *de Andalucía*	Oporto, Portugal	M1790 blue
I/ *de Galicia*	Setúbal, Portugal	M1805 white
II/ *de Galicia*	Setúbal, Portugal	M1802 blue

The grenadier companies were permanently separated from their parent units and combined into four *Divisiónes de Granaderos Provinciales* (Provincial Grenadier Regiments) each with two battalions of 600 men named *Castilla la Vieja* (Old Castile), *Castilla la Nueva* (New Castile), *Andalusia* and *Galicia*. By 1808 the units were at or near full strength of about 550 men.[140]

Grenadier company:
1 *capitán*, 2 *tenientes* [, 2 *subtenientes*, 1 *sargento primero*, 4 *sargentos segundos*, 3 *tambores*, 8 *cabos primeros*, 8 *cabos segundos*, 128 *granaderos*.

The *inspector general de milicias* Pedro Mendiueta report[141] dated 16 May 1808 stated that the *Granaderos Provinciales* wore M1790 blue (2 Bns), M1802 blue (1 Bn), M1805 white (2 Bns) and the final Bn had no serviceable uniform (see p280).

Provincial Militia Grenadier in M1790 uniform
[After Bueno]

---

[140] Oman (1902) 89 & 92; Partridge & Oliver (1998) p299
[141] Mendinueta (16 May 1808) *Noticia de las Provincias y Destinos que tienen en ellas los 8 Batallones de las 4 Divisiones de Granaderos y los 42 Regimientos de Milicias….., Madrid.

Cuerpo de Inválidos Hábiles (Invalid Corps)

The Invalid Corps consisted of 41 of veteran soldiers for garrison and police duties in various forts and cities.[142]

1805

Cuerpo de Inválidos Hábiles

After Bueno

New Castile: *Madrid* (4 coys), *Aranjuez* (1 coy).

Old Castile: *Ciudad Rodrigo* (2 coys), *Santander* (1 coy), *Canal de Campos* (1 coy), *San Felices* (1 coy), *Puebla de Sanabria* (1 coy) *Real Sitio de San Ildefonso* (1 coy).

Valencia: In the Citadel (2 coys), *Denia* (1 coys), *Peñíscala* (1 coy).

Navarre: *Pamplona* (3 coys), *Fuemerrabía* (1 coys).

Andalucía: *Seville* (1 coy), *Tarifa* (1 coy), *Granada* (1 coy), *Motril* (1 coy), *Almuñécar* (1 coy), *Marbella* (1 coy), *Adra* (1 coy), *Nerja* (1 coy), *Almería* (2 coys), *Almadén* (1 coy).

Galicia: *Tuy* (2 coys), *Bayona* (1 coy), *Monterrey* (1 coy).

Extremadura: *Badajóz* (1 coy), *Valencia de Alcántara* (1 coy), *Alburquerque* (1 coy) and *Alcántara* (3 coys).

Uniform

HEADWEAR: Bicorn and white hat lace in 1801.

TUNIC: Blue coat with blue collar and lapels, white cuffs, and white turnbacks.

WAISTCOAT: White waistcoat.

BUTTONS: White metal buttons.

LEGWEAR: Mid to dark blue breeches, white gaiters and blacke shoes.

Cuerpo de Inválidos Hábiles, 1805
Reglamento de Uniformidad del Ejercito y la Marina en 1805

[142] Bueno (1982) p17 and Nafziger (1993) p3.

Milicias Urbanas (Urban Militia)

This was the second reserve in the army of Carlos IV and had 114 companies whose primary role was to enforce public order. They served as garrisons of various cities with inferior quality troops and equipment.[143]

Table 11: *Milicias Urbanas* (Urban Militia)

City	Established	Companies
Alburquerque	1762	8 coys
Alcántara	1762	6 coys
Alconchel	1762	1 coy
Badajóz	1762	14 coys
Cádiz	1762	20 coys
Campo de Gibraltar	1762	13 coys
Cartagena	1762	9 coys
Ceuta	1762	5 coys
Ciudad Rodrigo	1768	6 coys
La Coruña	1766	12 coys
Puerto de Santa María	1762	9 coys
Tarifa	1769	4 coys
Valencia de Alcántara	1766	7 coys

1790

Cadiz   Puerto de Santa Maria

Milicias Urbanas

After Bueno

---

[143] Bueno (1982) 16-17 and Nafziger (1993) p3

1807

Cadiz, captain **Tarifa, captain**

Milicia Urbanas
After Bueno

Batallón De Milicias Urbanas de Ciudad Rodrigo

Created in 1767 with nine companies commanded by the Garrison Commander, when it was presented with two flags that it carried until 1810 (despite the 1802 regulations that reduced the number of flags to one). The white linen flag measuring 160cm by 166cm painted as follows:[144]

> *Obverse*: City Rodrigo shield consisting of three columns surmounted by a plinth on blue field and ducal crown and bordered with two blue and two red flags. Around these in red letters: "*POR LA RELIJION / POR EL REY / Y / POR LA PATRIA.*"
>
> *Reverse*: The same as obverse except the inscription was "*CIUDAD RODRIGO.*"

---

[144] Sorando Muzás (2000) CD, p48-49

Compañías Fijas (Garrison Coys)

These were stationed in the various fortresses around Spain.[145]

Andalucía: *Escopeteros de Getares* and *Infantería* (Est. 1705) at Campo de Gibraltar, ten *Compañías de la Costa de Granada* (Est. 1492 and re-organised in 1716)[146], *Escopeteros de Andalucía* (2 coys) (Est. 1776),

Aragón: *Compañía Suelta de Fusileros* (Est. 1766).

Castile: *Compañía Suelta de Castilla* (Est. 1792).

Catalonia: *Compañía Fija de Infantería de la Plaza de Rosas.*

Ceuta: *Compañía de Caballería de Lanzas de Ceuta* (Est. 1584), *Compañía Fijas de Moros Mogataces* (Est. 1734 in Oran, Algeria), *Fijas de los Tres Presidios Menores de Melilla, Peñón de Vélez de la Gomera y Alhucemas* and *Alhucemas.*

Levante: *Compañía Suelta de Escopeteros* in Valencia.

Compañía Suelta de Fusileros (Est. 1766)
Reglamento de Uniformidad del Ejercito y la Marina en 1805

**Compañía Fijas de Moros Mogataces
[Est. 1734 in Oran, Algeria], 1805**
Reglamento de Uniformidad del Ejercito y la Marina en 1805

---

145 Bueno (1 982) p17; Cano Velasco (1984) IV: pp13-18; Hernández Pardo (1984) V: pp128-132
146 Ten companies of *Infantería Fija de la Costa de Granada* were formed in 1762 under the name of *Milicias Urbanas* (Urban Militia) before being renamed on 24 February 1780. The 11th Coy was formed in 1799.

Escopeteros
de Getares

Compañía de la
Costa de Granada

Compañías Sueltas
del Campo de Gibraltar

Compañía de Caballería
de Lanzas de Ceuta

Officer of Fijas de los Tres
Presidios Menores de Melilla

Compañías Fijas (Garrison Coys)

After Bueno

Bibliography

Arteche, Gómez de (1868) *Guerra de la Independencia*, Volume I, Madrid

Benninghoff II, Herman O. (1991) "Some Spanish Weapons in the American Revolution," *Bulletin of the American Society of Arms Collectors*, **91**, 1-9

Balagny (1902-07) *Campagne de l'Empereur Napoleon en Espagne (1808-09)*, Volume I, Paris

Brinckerhoff, Sidney B., and Pierce A. Chamberlain (1972). *Spanish Military Weapons in Colonial America, 1700-1821*, Stackpole Books

Boppe P. (1899 rp 1986) *Les Espagnols a la Grande Armée*, C. Terana Editeur

Brum, António de (1822) *Estados de la Organización y Fuerza de los Ejércitos Españoles Beligerantes en la Península, durante la Guerra de España contra Bonaparte*, Sección de Historia Militar, Ejército Español, Barcelona

Bueno Carrera, José María
- (1982) *El Ejército y la Armada en 1808*, Aldaba Militaría, Madrid
- (1989) *Uniformes Militares de la Guerra de la Independencia*, Aldaba Militaría, Madrid
- (1990) *La Expedición Española a Dinamarca 1807-1808*, Aldaba Militaría, Madrid
- (1991) *Andalucía y sus Milicias*, Aldaba Militaría, Madrid

Calvó Pascal, Juan L.
- (1980) *Armas Blancas para Tropa en la Caballería Española*, Asociación El Cid
- (2008) *Armamento Español en la Guerra de la Independencia*, Ministerio de Defensa, Madrid
- (2011) *Armaments of the Troops of the Royal Household 1788-1931*, Private publication, (translation of *Armamento de las Tropas de Casa Real, 1788-1931*)

Cano Velasco, Fernando (1984) *Historia de las Fuerzas Armadas*, Volume IV – Guardia Civil, Ediciones Palafox, Zaragoza

Chartrand, R.
- (1998), *The Spanish Army of the Napoleonic Wars (1) 1793-1808*, Osprey
- (1999), *The Spanish Army of the Napoleonic Wars (2) 1808-1812*, Osprey
- (1999), *The Spanish Army of the Napoleonic Wars (3) 1812-1815*, Osprey
- (2011), *The Spanish Army in North America 1700-1783*, Osprey

Clonard, Conde de (1851-59) *Historia orgánica de las armas de Infantería y caballería españolas*, Volumes V-XVI, Madrid

Coppens B., Courcelle P., Petard P. and Lordey D.(1997) *Les Uniformes des Guerres Napoléoniennes*, Volume 1 French and Allied Troops, Editions Quatuor, France

Dempsey G.C.
- (2002) *Napoleon's Mercenaries: Foreign Units in the French Army under the Consulate and Empire 1799-1814*, Greenhill Books, London
- (2004), "Coin de l'Iconographie - le manuscrit du bourgeois de Hambourg Erschienen," *Soldats Napoléoniens*, Nr. 2

Digby Smith (Otto von Pivka)
- (1975) *Spanish Armies of the Napoleonic Wars*, Osprey
- (1979) *Armies of the Napoleonic Era*, David and Charles
- (1998) *The Greenhill Napoleonic Wars Data Book*, Greenhill Books

- (2013 and 2014) *Napoleon's German Division in Spain*, Volume I & II, Ken Trotman.

Esdaile C.J.
- (1988) *The Spanish Army in the Peninsular War*, Manchester University Press
- (1999) "Oman's History in its Spanish Context," In Paddy Griffith (ed). *A History of the Peninsular War*, Volume IX – Modern Studies of the War in Spain, 1808-1814, Greenhill Books, London, pp299-315
- (2002) *The Peninsular War: a New History*, Allen Lane, London
- (2008) "Conscriptions in Spain in the Napoleonic era," in Donald Stoker, Frederick Schneid and Harold Blanton (eds)., *Conscription in Napoleonic Europe 1789-1815: A Revolution in Military Affairs?*, Routledge, pp102-121
- (2011) "The Spanish Army," in G. Fremont Barnes (ed). *Armies of the Napoleonic Wars*, Pen and Sword, pp188-211
- (2012) *The Spanish Army in the Peninsular War*, 2nd Edition, Partisan Press

Espirito Santo, Gabriel (2012). *An Introduction to the Anglo-Portuguese Army Logistics in the Peninsular War*, Tribuna da Historia. Translated by Pedro de Brito.

Fuente, Francisco de la (2010) *Dom Miguel Pereira Forjaz, His career and Roile in the Mobilisation of the Portuguese Army and Defense of Portugal during the Peninsular War, 1807-1814*, Tribuna da Historia

Goddard T. and Booth J. (1812) *The military costume of Europe; exhibited in a series of highly-finished military figures, in the uniform of their several corps; with a concise description, and historical anecdotes; forming memoirs of the various armies of the present time.* London, 2 Volumes (96 plates)

Godchot (1924) *Les Espagnols du Marquis de la Romana 1807-1808*, Paris

Grant, Charles (2009) *Wellington's Return, The Battle of Talavera 1809*, Partizan Press

Guerrero Acosta, José M. (2009) *Memorias de Soldados Españoles durante la Guerra de la Independencia (1806-1815)*, Ministerio de Defensa, Madrid
- Capitán Rafael de Lanza y de Valls (1806-1813) "Memorias de Don Rafael de Llanza y de Valls, Capitán del Antiguo Regimiento de Infantería de Guadalajara: Toscana – Dinamarca – Francia –Rusia –España," pp67-118
- Almansa Diary (1807-1811) "Cuaderno de Ruta General de Tropas de Nuestro Ejército durante la Guerra de la Independencia por la Península," pp137-184

Haythornthwaite, P.J.
- (1978) *Uniforms of the Peninsular Wars 1807-14*, Blandford Press
- (1988) *Napoleon's Military Machine*, Guild Publishing, London

Redondo del Pozo, Luís (ed). (1983) *Historia de las Fuerzas Armadas*, Volume II – Las Armas y los Servicos, Ediciones Palafox, Zaragoza

Hernández Pardo, Pedro (ed). (1984) *Historia de las Fuerzas Armadas*, Volume V, Ediciones Palafox, Zaragoza

Johnston, R.M. ed. (2002) *In the Words of Napoleon; The Emperor Day to Day*, Greenhill Books

Knötel, Richard (1904), *Mitteilungen zur Geschichte der Militärischen Tracht: Das grosse Uniformwerk des Hamburgers Christoph Suhr 1806-1815*, Verlag von Max Bab, Berlin

Laborde, Alexander de (1809) *A View of Spain comprising a Descriptive Itinerary of each Province and a General Statistical Account of the Country*, Longman, London (Translated from French edition of Laborde (1808) *Itinéraire descriptif de l'Espagne...*, Paris

Lefebvre, G. (1969) *Napoleon from Tilsit to Waterloo*, Routledge and Kegan Paul, London (Translation from French of the 1936 edition by J.E. Anderson)

Lienhart and Humbert (1895) *Uniformes de l'Armée Francaise*, Volume 5, Leipzig

Margin, M. de (1902) *Représentation des uniformes de toutes les troupes qui ont été casernées à Hambourg, de l'année 1806 a l'année 1815. Reproduction de l'album dit: "Manuscrit du brugeois de Hambourg"*, M. Terrel des Chenes, Paris (155 numbered copies)

Martins, Paul (1968) *European Military Uniforms*, Hamlyn

Mendinueta, Pedro (16 May 1808) *Noticia de las Provincias y Destinos que tienen en ellas los 8 Batallones de las 4 Divisiones de Granaderos y los 42 Regimientos de Milicias. Con Expresión de la Fuerza de su Instituto, la que falta para su Complete, y el estado de uso del Vestuario y Armamento de cada uno*, Madrid. This report was by Pedro Mendiueta (1736-1825) who was *inspector general de milicias* and member of the Supreme Council of War.

Moreno Alonso, Manuel (2008) *La batalla de Bailén: el surgimiento de una nación*, Sílex ediciones, Madrid

Nafziger GF (1993) *The Armies of Spain and Portugal*, 3rd Edition, The Nafziger Collection

Navas Ramírez-Cruzado, José (2008) "El Ejército Español," *La Guerra de la Independencia Española: Un visión militar*, Volume 1, pp119-134

Oman C, (1902-1930), *History of the Peninsular War*, Volume I-VII, London

Ordovás, Juan Josef (1807) *Estado del Ejército y la Armada de Su Majestad Católica formado por el Teniente Coronel del Real Cuerpo de Ingenieros Don Juan José Ordovás, año 1807*, Madrid.

Palmer, Alan (1990) *Bernadotte*, London

Partridge R. and Oliver M. (1999) *Napoleonic Army Handbook: The British Army and her Allies*, Constable

Pacquette, Gabriel B. (2011) *Enlightenment, Governance and Reform in Spain and its Enpire, 1759-1808,* Palgrave Macmillan

Pigeaud A. (1998) "Le Bourgeois de Hambourg," *Tradition Hors Série* Nr. 5

Redondo Díaz, Fernando (ed). (1983) *Historia de las Fuerzas Armadas*, Volume I - Historia bélica de España, Ediciones Palafox, Zaragoza

Reglamento lithographs (1805 and 1806) *Reglamento de Uniformidad del Ejército y la Marina en 1805*, Madrid. Each has about 100 lithographs showing the new M1805 uniform.

Rodríguez J.M. (2005) "Pedro Caro y Sureda, 3rd Marqués de la Romana," www.napoleon-series.org/research/biographies/c_Romana.html, (Accessed 21/11/2009)

Rubí, B.B. (1976) *Armamento Portátil Español 1764-1939*, San Martín

Sanudo J. J. (1999) "Oman's view of the Spanish Army in the Peninsular War Reassessed," in Paddy Griffith ed. (1999) *History of the Peninsular War*, Volume IX: Modern Studies of the War in Spain and Portugal, 1808-1814, Greenhill Books, pp145-160

Sapherson C.A. (1991) *Peninsular Armies 1808-14*, Raider Games

Soares Branco, Pedro (2007) *Os Uniformes Portugeses na Guerra Peninsular*, Tribuna da Historia.

Sorando Muzás, Luís
- (2001) *Banderas, estandartes y trofeos del Museo del Ejército 1700-1843, Catálogo razonado*, M. Defensa

- (Dec 2007) "L'Infanterie de ligne espagnole en 1808," *Soldats Napoléoniens*, No. 16
- (2008) "Banderas de las Tropas españolas durante la Guerra de la Independencia"in *La Guerra de la Independencia (1808-1814), el pueblo español, su ejército y sus aliados frente a la ocupación napoleónica*, M. Defensa, pp. 324- 337.
- (1 Oct 2012) "La Infantería de Línea Española en 1808," *Miniatures Militares Blog*, http://miniaturasmilitaresalfonscanovas.blogspot.co.uk
- (2012) "La Infantería de Línea Española en 1808," *Miniatures Militares*

Stein, M. (June 2007), "Uniformserie Suhr," *Napoleon Online*, www.Napoleon-online.de/suhr.html, (Accessed on 1 November 2009)

Stiot, R.D. (1973) "Monographie des Éditions de l'Album du Bourgeois de Hambourg. Erschienen," *Carnet de la Sabretache*, New Series, Nr. 19

Suhr C.
- (1808) *Die Spanischen Truppen der Division Romana in Hamburg während der Jahre 1807 und 1808*, Hamburg (18 plates Courtesy of the Berlin Art Library and Photographs by Markus Stein of Napoleon-Online)
- (1818) *Das Brokthor in Hamburg Während der Belagerungszeit 1813-14*, Hamburg
- (1820) *Abbildung der Uniformen aller in Hamburg seit den Jahren 1806 bis 1815 einquartirt gewesener Truppen*, Hamburg

Suhr C. and H. Achard (rp1970), *Manuscrit du Bourgeois de Hambourg*, S.I., Paris, 2 Volumes

Taylor B. (2006) *The Empire of the French: A Chronology of the Revolutionary and Napoleonic Wars 1792-1815*, Spellmount

Windrow M. and Embleton G. (1974) *Military Dress of the Peninsular War*, Ian Allen

Wise T. (1978) *Flags of the Napoleonic Wars*, Volume 3, Osprey

Index